THE GREEN LEAP

The publisher gratefully acknowledges the generous support of the
Ralph and Shirley Shapiro Endowment Fund in Environmental Studies of
the University of California Press Foundation.

THE GREEN LEAP

A PRIMER FOR CONSERVING BIODIVERSITY
IN SUBDIVISION DEVELOPMENT

Mark E. Hostetler

UNIVERSITY OF CALIFORNIA PRESS

Berkeley Los Angeles London

University of California Press, one of the most distinguished
university presses in the United States, enriches lives around
the world by advancing scholarship in the humanities, social
sciences, and natural sciences. Its activities are supported by
the UC Press Foundation and by philanthropic contributions
from individuals and institutions. For more information, visit
www.ucpress.edu.

University of California Press
Berkeley and Los Angeles, California

University of California Press, Ltd.
London, England

Library of Congress Cataloging-in-Publication Data

Hostetler, Mark E.
    The green leap : a primer for conserving biodiversity in
subdivision development / Mark E. Hostetler.
        p.   cm.
    Includes bibliographical references and index.
    ISBN 978-0-520-27110-4 (cloth : alk. paper)
    ISBN 978-0-520-27111-1 (pbk. : alk. paper)
    1. Planned communities—Environmental aspects.
2. New towns—Environmental aspects.   3. Urban ecology
(Biology)   4. Biodiversity conservation.   I. Title
    HT169.55.H67   2012
    307.76'8—dc23

                                              2011033762

Manufactured in the United States of America

21   20   19   18   17   16   15   14   13   12
10   9   8   7   6   5   4   3   2   1

In keeping with a commitment to support environmentally
responsible and sustainable printing practices, UC Press
has printed this book on 50-pound Enterprise, a 30% post-
consumer-waste, recycled, deinked fiber that is processed
chlorine-free. It is acid-free and meets all ANSI/NISO (z 39.48)
requirements.

To my wife, son, and daughter, Meryl, Jamm, and Tupelo, who are a source of inspiration, love, and support—our family hikes and travels help me to celebrate the intricate connections between humans and nature

And to my parents, Keith and Jeanette, who nurtured my love of the outdoors and instilled in me a desire to make a difference

CONTENTS

BOXED TEXTS

PREFACE AND ACKNOWLEDGMENTS

We stand now where two roads diverge. But unlike the roads in Robert Frost's familiar poem, they are not equally fair. The road we have long been traveling is deceptively easy, a smooth superhighway on which we progress with great speed, but at its end lies disaster. The other fork of the road—the one less traveled by—offers our last, our only chance to reach a destination that assures the preservation of the earth.

—Rachel Carson, author and conservationist

The green leap is actually a big leap: conventional development is like a huge barge going down a river—it will take some effort to change its direction, because today's development has years of inertia behind it. Conventional thinking about how development occurs is shaped by economics, codes and regulations, politics, societal values, and past successes. Some people have become complacent about the way communities grow and how they look. From homeowners and developers to policy makers, collectively we have set in motion a system of checks and balances that has resulted in neighborhoods dominated by turf, exotic plants, and very little open space. It's not that we are trying to wipe out the environmental assets in and around urban areas; we are simply caught up in the conventional process of laying down roads, turf, and homes in a manner that has been shaped by historical trends. Municipalities have a number of regulatory hoops that developers must jump through in order to have their projects approved, and a host of environmental consultants and developers have become comfortable with this planning process. Even in our neighborhoods, societal norms sometimes dictate that front yards must contain uniform turf and pavement areas that stretch alongside neighborhood roads. Against this cultural and institutional background, unique ideas tend to be squashed because the conventional evaluation procedures, policies, and way of thinking have become an accepted lens through which we view homes, yards, and neighborhoods. To conserve many of our native plants and animals, we will have to adopt a new lens and develop a new way to create and maintain urban communities. This lens is sustainability, and the backdrop to the concept of sustainability is biodiversity.

Why conserve biodiversity? The reasons range from people's desire to view native plants and animals in their own communities to the environmental, social, health, and economic services that biodiverse ecosystems provide (e.g., they filter stormwater, and they are places for recreation, reduction of stress, and ecotourism). Each of us has a connection to nature; and across the globe, people enjoy the green aspects of an urban area, including trees, shrubs, flowers, and wildlife. Every area is distinct, and indigenous (native) plants and animals give us a sense of place and pride in our local communities. Urban environments are an important component of the biodiversity issue— not only do they affect the plants, animals, and other organisms found within a city's limits, but they also affect natural habitat tens or even thousands of miles away. How every neighborhood is designed and managed determines the degree of this effect. A combination of decisions by policy makers, developers, and residents shapes our ability to conserve natural resources over the short and the long term. Will future generations be able to experience the unique assortment of flora and fauna that we experience today?

Urban communities can be designed and managed for biodiversity, not only conserving and restoring habitat for a variety of plant and animals within a neighborhood, but also—and most important—minimizing our impact on surrounding natural areas. Hearing or viewing an array of birds, and watching the excitement of children observing different critters, are events that add value to any community. Increasingly, what we do within our own neighborhoods has important ramifications for the health of regional plant and animal populations. Our streams, lakes, wetlands, forests, prairies, coastal environments, and other natural environments are all affected by the activities that happen within the metropolitan area. Nothing we do is contained within an urban boundary. We know this because we are continually confronted by stories about the degradation of our lakes, streams, coasts, and forests from urban stormwater runoff and invasive exotic plants and animals that have escaped from urban areas and spread into natural areas. Even the way we design and operate our homes and yards can affect global climate change. The net amount of CO_2 produced is a result of energy consumed to maintain our homes and yards minus CO_2 taken up by the vegetation we have in our yards.

The primary purpose of this book is to shift the barge—that is, conventional development—to a different course by presenting the dynamic roles of policy makers, developers, and the public and the actions each can take to create sustainable communities. Any individual or organization that strives to conserve biodiversity must have a plan that engages all of these stakeholders. With such a conservation strategy in place, urban areas will contain functional, habitats for plants and animals and cities will reduce their negative impact on surrounding lands. However, current conservation efforts directed at the process of subdividing land often are piecemeal; they do not entail a holistic strategy that effectively uses policy, engages built environment professionals, and involves the general public. I present several design and management practices that can be adopted to help create and maintain biodiverse communities, including specific tactics that policy makers, developers, and neighborhood residents can employ to increase both the uptake of conservation practices and their long-term success. This book is useful for planning the construction of new subdivisions and for helping retrofit existing yards and neighborhoods. Almost any community can adopt fairly simple practices to address biodiversity and natural resource conservation. And the cumulative impact can be remarkable when these practices are adopted by a number of policy makers, developers, and homeowners.

As a wildlife ecologist, I have a keen interest in urban environments and in the creation of green communities, because, even with a city's best attempts to preserve natural areas and processes, success happens only if these conservation actions are linked to people's daily activities within their homes, yards, and neighborhoods. The information contained in this book does have roots in academic studies, but most of it derives from my attempts to apply research-based information to the "real world." In 2004, I helped form an academic group at the University of Florida called the Program for Resource Efficient Communities (www.buildgreen.ufl.edu). This program is composed of scientists from different disciplines, and our main mission is to serve as a portal to the university that lets municipalities, developers, and residents obtain advice and guidance on how to create functioning green communities. We frequently meet with developers and municipalities to discuss the best design and management options available when creating a green community. Often, what we thought were easy solutions to reduce energy and water consumption, or to conserve biodiversity, were in reality difficult to put into practice. Barriers can materialize throughout the development process, and they take many forms. Sometimes complex political and governmental rules and perceptions, and even a lack of basic trust among governmental departments, are enough to hinder the adoption of the best design and management practices. Other times, economics, social and cultural factors, or even the unavailability of recommended technologies can stop a project in its tracks. As I noted earlier, development has been traveling the same course for a long time—the past sixty years, in fact—and charting a new one takes a coordinated effort by the different sectors of society. My hope is that this book will provide insights into how to shift our current course.

This book would not have been possible without the multitude of interactions I've had with my academic colleagues, students, and various built environment practitioners throughout Florida and around the world. Current and previous graduate students whom I have had the privilege of advising have conducted top-notch research and outreach projects, producing some illuminating ideas about and insights into constructing green communities. Many of the ideas contained within this book evolved from my experiences related to the Program for Resource Efficient Communities, and I am indebted to my colleagues in this program. Many thanks to Pierce Jones, Hal Knowles, Michael Dukes, Glenn Acomb, Mark Clark, and Kathleen Ruppert, as well as to a host of other staff members and students associated with the program. In addition, I thank Colin Meurk and the folks at Landcare Research, New Zealand, where I spent a wonderful year and formulated the beginnings of the book.

My spouse, Meryl Klein, has been a source of inspiration and support and, as an environmental educator herself, has provided ideas and feedback that have helped shape this book. Thanks also to Leslie Klein and Jeanette Hostetler for helping to edit the book. And always in the back of my mind are my two little ones, my son, Jámm, and daughter, Tupelo. It is amazing to watch children grow and explore their environment. Our yard is the place both of my kids first began to interact with wildlife; in particular, Jámm has developed a passion for catching frogs, lizards, and bugs—of course asking me hundreds of questions along the way. I cannot help but think about what type of world they will encounter when they reach adulthood, and I hope this book will help shape the creation of healthy and functional green communities in which my own children and future generations will live.

PART ONE

Key Principles and Players

Imagine this, a gathering of policy makers, environmental consultants, developers, landowners, and members of the public, all assembled in a room to discuss a land use change to make way for a proposed residential development. The focus, though, is how to make it a green development, and everybody in the room is interested in creating a community that is livable, walkable, and energy-efficient, and which conserves biodiversity. Speaker after speaker stands up to discuss a particular topic and makes a case for this issue or that issue. Typically a land use map is displayed on a screen, and a heated but cordial discussion ensues about where, within the subdivision, the roads and homes should go and where open space should be conserved. Many buzzwords and concepts are thrown about: *smart growth, sustainability, conservation subdivision, pedestrian-friendly, wildlife corridors, biodiversity conservation, Energy Star homes, low-impact development,* and *new urbanism.* At the end of this workshop, recommendations are made to the developers and their planning team. They go back to the drawing board and, months later, come back with a detailed map that shows the juxtaposition of roads, buildings, and open space. Many of the suggestions in the workshop have been incorporated into the design, and this design is ultimately passed by the planning board and elected officials. A development order is issued and the developers begin construction.

During the construction phase, the construction site manager, contractors, subcontractors, landscape architects, and civil engineers fully support the goal of conserving biodiversity, and they understand sustainable construction techniques that minimize impacts on conserved natural areas. They also install native plants in yards and common areas. The routes for earthwork machines are strictly controlled, and construction activities are geared to conserving natural areas both on built lots and in identified natural areas. To help with long-term management by residents, the developers' team has created an environmental education program to engage residents in conserving biodiversity. The developer has also implemented property deed restrictions that address biodiversity conservation, particularly how homeowners should manage their yards and open spaces. Homeowners are very interested in conserving biodiversity, and they have formed nature clubs and have organized restoration activities to improve upon what the developer has started. The homeowners association helps inform residents about biodiversity conservation, and the association plays an active role in managing the natural areas and informing residents about proper yard management. Overall, each homeowner becomes a steward of the land, and the neighborhood culture is one that values biodiversity conservation.

Is there anything wrong with the above scenario? Sounds pretty good—no? The first problem is the simple fact that this type of sustainable-development discussion is uncommon, and that, more often than not, conventional subdivisions are created. Constructing conventional subdivisions is typically the easiest path as a result of current policies, regulations, perceptions about the marketplace, and just plain inertia. Second, where green-development discussions do occur, 95 percent of the emphasis is on design; almost none is placed on construction and long-term management. While design is important, equally important are the ways a site is managed during construction and, most significant, how residents manage their homes, yards, and neighborhoods once they move in. I have seen even the best designs go awry once a host of contractors and subcontractors has implemented a plan, and once an assortment of people with different backgrounds has moved into a community! Construction and postconstruction issues are of particular concern; the very survival of the plants and animals is contingent on the way a construction site is managed and how engaged the local residents are in terms of biodiversity conservation.

This book is meant to help policy makers, developers, other built environment professionals, and residents to create and maintain *functional*, urban developments that conserve biodiversity. Information in this book primarily pertains to land that has already been zoned for development, and I spend little time on strategies to determine where, across a county, developable land, versus conserved land, should be located. While this is an essential topic, it is beyond the scope of this book. How developments are designed, built, and managed has important ramifications for biodiversity conservation throughout any region. Thus, this book focuses on issues and conservation practices related to the creation and maintenance of subdivisions.

I divided the book into two parts. The first gives background information about green communities and biodiversity, addressing two important questions: why is it important to conserve biodiversity, and who are the players and decision makers who make or break a functioning, green community? This discussion is critical because urban biodiversity conservation depends on whether policy makers, developers, and residents are engaged and explicitly involved. It also provides the foundation for principles and practices suggested in the latter part of the book. Part 2 focuses on land parcels marked for development, and on specific issues and practices that can be adopted to improve biodiversity when land is subdivided.

I assume that readers of this book are already interested in biodiversity conservation. The book is a primer, and it is my hope that readers will come away with a better understanding of specific design and management practices, and of the unique roles the policy makers, the developers, and the public play in the creation and maintenance of urban biodiversity. Information in this book is also useful for sustainability classes, natural resource conservation classes, and academic design studios, because training environmentalists, policy makers, architects, environmental engineers, and landscape architects is crucial to the implementation of successful biodiversity conservation strategies. Such education will, I hope, increase the number of green development discussions and ultimately improve the conservation of native species and habitats.

Biodiversity is generally defined as the variety of life. Biodiversity is a global concept but can refer to the number of habitats and species within a local area or region. It is not an exact term and can have various interpretations, but it usually has three components.

- *Ecosystem diversity.* The earth has a wide variety of ecosystems where life exists. Ecosystems are basically interacting associations of microbes, plants, animals, and their physical environment within a defined space. Deserts, coral reefs, and tropical rain forests are just a few types of ecosystems.
- *Species diversity.* When people refer to biodiversity, they typically mean species diversity. This is the number of different types of organisms, including plants and animals, in a given area.

• *Genetic diversity*. This is the variety of genetic information contained in all the individual plants, animals, and microorganisms. It occurs within and between populations of species as well as between individual species. For example, the Florida panther (*Puma concolor coryi*) and Texas cougar (*Puma concolor stanleyana*) are two subspecies of the mountain lion. Even the genetic makeup of a species of plant differs according to the locality in which the plant is found.

When speaking of biodiversity conservation, it is important to distinguish between biodiversity and species richness. Biodiversity is a measure of the variety of species or ecosystems found naturally in an area (i.e., indigenous, or native, species) or found nowhere else in the world (i.e., endemic species). Some areas have a disproportionately large numbers of endemics; for example, the California Floristic Province has about twenty-one hundred endemic plant species (www.biodiversityhotspots.org). Species richness is simply a count of the number of different species within a defined area, and this number can contain exotic species. An *exotic* species is typically defined as an organism recently introduced to an area by humans. If we replaced the twenty-one hundred endemic species of the California Floristic Province with five thousand exotic species, then the total species richness would, in fact, become greater in this region. But while that area's species richness would increase to five thousand species, the world's biodiversity would actually decline by twenty-one hundred very important species. Packing in more species doesn't increase biodiversity—it merely spreads globally common species to more places, sometimes at the expense of local plants and animals.

CHAPTER I

Why Build Biodiverse Communities?

The conservation of our natural resources and their proper use constitute the funda-
mental problem which underlies almost every other problem of our national life.
—Theodore Roosevelt

Why worry about urban biodiversity? Why not just concentrate on biodiversity conservation outside the boundaries of cities? First, the millions of people who make daily decisions in urban environments can have huge impacts on local and regional natural resources. We have crossed a threshold around the world: more than 50 percent of the world's population resides in urban areas.[1] Over the past century, we have learned that local decisions have global consequences and global decisions have local impacts. Building communities takes a vast amount of natural resources; think about the energy required to make and transport building materials to create homes, roads, and landscapes within a given community. Then think about how we live in these communities: we heat and cool our homes, drive from one place to another, consume food, and maintain our yards. All of this takes energy, in the form of electricity and liquid fuel. Energy has to come from somewhere, and today, most of our energy is derived from fossil fuel sources (coal, natural gas, oil). Mining for coal, and drilling for oil and natural gas, affects our land, air, and water. The construction and maintenance of cities is contingent on the consumption of natural resources gathered from local, regional, and global locations. Calculating the ecological footprint is a popular scientific technique that determines the amount of land and marine area required both to supply the resources a human population consumes and to absorb and dispose of the corresponding waste this consumption generates.[2] In the United States, the biocapacity, or the amount of land available to support the population, is less than the

TABLE I   ECOLOGICAL FOOTPRINT AND BIOCAPACITY OF NORTH
AMERICAN COUNTRIES IN 2005

Country	Population (Million)	Ecological Footprint (Hectares per Person)	Biocapacity (Hectares per Person)	Ecological Deficit or Reserve (Hectares per Person)
United States	298.2	9.4	5.0	−4.4
Canada	32.3	7.1	20.0	+13.9
Mexico	107.0	3.4	1.7	−1.7

SOURCE: Global Footprint Network. 2005. "Ecological Footprint and Biocapacity," www.footprintnetwork.org.

amount of land needed to satisfy current consumption rates (Table 1). So the country is operating at a deficit and will need to find additional land outside its borders to gather the required resources to meet current consumption levels.

How is biodiversity conservation linked to natural resource consumption? Often, the incorporation of biodiversity principles into growth management strategies has the added benefit of reducing natural resource consumption. For instance, the use of native plants and ecologically minded construction techniques to conserve topsoil and existing trees can reduce water and energy consumption and decrease the impacts of residential growth on nearby environments. In landscaping, topsoil conservation and the use of native plants instead of nonnative turf often lead to a reduced need for irrigation, fertilizers, and pesticides.[3] In combination with a reduction of impervious surfaces such as asphalt, and the use of more trees to intercept rainfall, such efforts lead to reduced stormwater runoff and fewer pollutants being carried to nearby wetlands.[4] In neighborhoods, conserved trees help shade homes during the summer, reducing energy needed to cool a home.[5] Conserving urban biodiversity will pay strong dividends to the reduction of natural resource consumption simply because the world's urban population is only going to increase.[6]

In addition, when people have their first or primary experience with nature in their own yards and neighborhoods, an opportunity exists for them to feel a connection with the land, and this can generate a multitude of environmental stewards. Urban neighborhoods and workplaces are where people recreate, interact with friends, spend money, consume resources, and generally spend the majority of their time. Unfortunately, biodiversity in urban areas tends to be minimal, and the species that we see in urban areas are often nonnative and can be seen from one city to the next.[7] Because of this homogenization, urban denizens encounter few of their local plants and animals and become disconnected from their natural heritage. Daily contact with a limited diversity of native species and habitats promotes a sense that biodiversity is not that important to people living in cities. If decision makers, such as elected officials, urban policy makers, and developers, see the current state of urban environments and presume it is as it should be, they will continue to implement design and management strategies that do not incorporate biodiversity principles.[8] Case in point: open space conservation continues to be undervalued and plays second fiddle to other socioeconomic concerns.[9] The experience in a homogenized urban environment can lead to environmental amnesia from one generation to the next. Children who grow up in cities with little biodiversity become accustomed to these environments and, as a result, place little importance on the decline of natural environments that surround their neighborhoods.[10] Ultimately, urban opportunities to experience and understand local natural heritage will promote a conservation ethic.[11]

The ecological integrity of natural areas is directly and indirectly affected by nearby cities. Urban growth fragments the natural environment, and such fragmentation can lead to the disappearance of sensitive animal and plant species. For example, the gopher tortoise (*Gopherus polyphemus*) is a species of special concern in many states, because its population has declined over the years as urban and agricultural development has destroyed its habitat.[12] Even the design and management of urban landscapes can have significant impacts on surrounding lands that house certain species like the gopher tortoise. With landscaped yards, there is a risk that nonnative plants may spread and become established in surrounding natural habitats. Called invasive exotics, these nonnative plants have frequently originated in urban areas—for example, several invasive exotic plant species have spread from their original locations in urban areas in California.[13] The maintenance of lawns and exotic horticultural plantings often requires the use of an array of pesticides, fertilizers, and herbicides. Fertilizers affect rivers, streams, and lakes by raising the levels of nitrates and phosphates, ultimately contributing to algal blooms,[14] fish kills,[15] coastal dead zones,[16] and the spread of invasive exotic plants.[17]

Recognizing that cities are primary areas through which people interact with and have an effect on nature, a group of scientists from around the world produced a unique document called the Erfurt Declaration (Box 1). This declaration is a good summary of the significance of urban biodiversity conservation. With well-designed and well-managed urban areas, biodiversity within a city's boundaries can be increased and detrimental impacts on surrounding

Box 1. The Erfurt Declaration—2008

Called the Erfurt Declaration, this document came from a 2008 international conference, "Urban Biodiversity and Design: Implementing the Convention on Biological Diversity in Towns and Cities," which took place May 21 through 24, 2008, in
Erfurt, Germany. Following is the exact wording of the document. The Erfurt Declaration also can be accessed from URBIO (www.fh-erfurt.de/urbio).

1. Preamble

The increasing urban population, climate change and loss of biodiversity are
all strongly connected. With two-thirds of a considerably larger world population
predicted to be living in urban areas by 2050, the "Battle for life on Earth" will be
lost or won in urban regions.

The role of urbanisation in the loss and degradation of global biodiversity was
acknowledged in the local Agenda 21 processes and in the Convention on Biological Diversity (CBD) in 1992 and has been discussed in the subsequent eight
Conferences of the Parties. Whilst cities pose major challenges for protecting biodiversity, the opportunities they offer have, so far, been understated.

A major step toward recognizing the potential of cities for biodiversity was
made in Curitiba (Brazil) in March 2007, when a global partnership in "Cities and
Biodiversity" was initiated by 34 mayors and numerous high level officials from
cities across all continents in order to engage local authorities to protect and sustain their unique contribution to global biodiversity.

From the 21st to 24th May 2008 in Erfurt (Germany) 400 scientists, planners
and other practitioners from around 50 countries summarized for the first time in
a global context the current scientific and practical approaches of implementing
the CBD in urban areas. This declaration reflects the views of the participants at
the "URBIO 2008" conference that urban biodiversity is a vital part of achieving the
aims of the Convention on Biological Diversity.

2. The importance of urban biodiversity

Urban biodiversity is the variety and richness of life including genetic, species
and habitat diversity found in and around towns and cities. During our "URBIO
2008" conference we discussed the current state of knowledge and practice in
"urban biodiversity". The contributions at the conference demonstrated clearly the
range of different approaches necessary to understand the importance and function
of urban biodiversity and to bring these into local practice. The approaches are:

- Investigation and evaluation of biodiversity in urban areas
- Cultural aspects of urban biodiversity
- Social aspects of urban biodiversity

- Urban biodiversity and climate change
- Design and future of urban biodiversity

Towns and cities are both important experimental areas and fields of experience in the interrelationship between humans and nature.

The case for urban biodiversity in relation to the aims of the CBD is compelling:

- Urban ecosystems have their own distinctive characteristics.
- Urban areas are centres of evolution and adaptation.
- Urban areas are complex hotspots and melting pots for regional biodiversity.
- Urban biodiversity can contribute significantly to the quality of life in an increasingly urban global society.
- Urban biodiversity is the only biodiversity that many people experience.

Experiencing urban biodiversity will be the key to halt the loss of global biodiversity, because people are more likely to take action for biodiversity if they have direct contact with nature.

3. Challenges for the future

Halting the global loss of biodiversity and ensuring all our cities are green, pleasant and prosperous places requires:

- Raising greater public awareness of biodiversity in urban areas
- Fostering interdisciplinary long-term research into urban biodiversity for a better understanding of the interactions between humans, urban biodiversity and global biodiversity
- Linking research on climate change and urban biodiversity
- Intensifying dialogues and establish a bridging mechanism between researchers, planners, policy makers and citizens to improve the integration of research findings into urban design
- Fostering education in urban biodiversity and design

Initiating new programs of activities concerning "Cities and Biodiversity" within the CBD would provide the mechanism needed to tackle these challenges.

To address these issues requires the following tasks and responsibilities:

- Scientific associations, networks and working groups should support international research networks on the importance of biodiversity in the urban context and its influence at regional and global scales.

(Continued on page 10)

- National and international institutions should support research and its translation into best practice for urban biodiversity and design.
- National governments and agencies for nature conservation should establish coordinating mechanisms. These should obtain, coordinate and monitor local and regional information concerning biodiversity and urbanization.
- Local authorities should link urban biodiversity with sustainable urban design.

As a community of urban biodiversity professionals we will especially support further CBD initiatives on "Cities and Biodiversity" through:

- Sharing our knowledge and commitment through this conference and in the future,
- establishing a global "URBIO" network for education and research into urban biodiversity,
- promoting urban biodiversity through continuing dialogue with the CBD especially, linking future urban biodiversity network—"URBIO"—meetings with future COP meetings.

---

land can be decreased. Such results promote the conservation of healthy, natural environments across a region, and this benefits not only society, public health, and the economy but also entire ecosystems.[18]

ECOSYSTEM BENEFITS

Civilization is not, as they often assume, the enslavement of a stable and constant earth. It is a state of mutual and interdependent cooperation between human animals, other animals, plants, and soils.

—Aldo Leopold

Urban, rural, and natural areas all interact in dynamic ways; and as stated earlier, what happens within urban areas affects the environment on local, regional, and global scales. Adopting practices that conserve the diversity of urban organisms can pay huge dividends for people. For example, the conservation of natural open space within the urban-rural matrix provides not only a sense of place and of beauty but also a wide variety of critical ecosystem services. Ecosystem services are the resources and processes, such as clean air and water, supplied by natural ecosystems, and these services are useful to humankind. These services, available free of charge, are highly valued economically, and yet they are rarely bought, sold, or factored into the cost of consumer goods and services. Once humans damage the ability of natural areas to provide these services, high costs to society are realized. Scientists around the world have collaborated and produced a nice summary of the consequences of ecosystem change on human well-being.[19] Ecosystem services are essentially the life support system for all species on earth, including humans. In a scientific paper published in the journal *Nature*,[20] the global economic value of twelve major ecosystem services and five major ecosystem goods was estimated to be approximately $16–54 trillion (U.S. dollars), with an average of $33 trillion (U.S. dollars) annually. The paper additionally estimated the global gross national product to be $18 trillion (U.S. dollars) annually for the services natural ecosystems provide.

The diversity of ecosystems, plants, insects, and animals benefits humans in a variety of ways.[21] For instance, wetlands help purify and remove contaminants from freshwater. Coastal wetlands serve as nurseries for many of the fish and shellfish species that we eat on a daily basis. Most medicines are derived from plant, fungal, and animal sources, and new sources of medicines are sometimes needed to advance our fight against diseases. If a species goes extinct, we lose its genetic material and our ability to derive new medicines from it. Pollination by animals helps in the production of food. A variety of insects and animals pollinate such crops as nuts, fruits, and vegetables,[22] but agriculture currently relies on one or two pollinating insects. Pollination is much more robust if there are many different species providing this service. In the United States, growers rely on European honey bees (*Apis mellifera*) for pollination of fruits, but the honey bee population is currently being decimated because of a number of factors, including parasitic mites and pesticides.[23] To pollinate citrus groves, farmers have relied on honey bee specialists who ship honey bee hives to each individual citrus grove. Because these managed hives are failing and honey prices have decreased, fewer people are shipping honey bee hives to local farmers. Farmers are scrambling to find adequate pollination services. Because the quantity and diversity of other insect pollinators have been reduced by the applications of pesticides and by habitat destruction,[24] local insect populations are insufficient to take over pollination services. Growers are now attempting to alter their agriculture practices and bring about the return of native pollinators.[25]

Habitat loss, another aspect of biodiversity loss, also can affect ecosystem services. The replacement of coastal ecosystems with development can lead to increased damage caused by tidal surges. When homes are built right on the coast, no buffer in the form of estuaries or dune ecosystems exists to protect human development from tidal surges, and often the beaches have to be rebuilt to save homes, at an enormous economic cost to the public. The Atlantic and Gulf states have spent upward of $2.5 billion to replenish beaches.[26] A highly diverse ecosystem is very good at producing the oxygen we breathe and at sequestering the carbon dioxide we produce in vast quantities through our consumption of fossil fuels.

Many intricate connections exist among the organisms in an ecosystem, and the loss of a few or many species can disrupt this balance and ultimately lead to a disruption in the service an ecosystem provides to us. Even managing pests can sometimes disrupt and alter natural processes, often with unintended consequences. For example, many species of birds serve as checks on insect populations that feed on tree foliage in forests, which we rely on for wood products. Models have predicted that, in the boreal forest, as the use of pesticides increased, forest foliage would become so dense that the populations of pest insects, such as spruce budworm, could not be effectively controlled by birds.[27] Pesticide use would be effective initially, but over time it would become ever more costly and ultimately ineffective because more and more pesticide would be required for the same effect. Eventually, huge insect outbreaks would occur and vast areas of forest would be affected. Thus, bird populations, along with judiciously applied pesticides, play an important role in controlling spruce budworms. If forest bird populations were to significantly decline, spruce budworm containment would become more and more difficult and economically infeasible.

What about loss of biodiversity in terms of species diversity? Could not exotic species that have replaced natives provide the same ecosystem services? Many exotic species can effectively remove CO_2, a greenhouse gas, from the atmosphere and sequester it. But homogenizing the species composition around the world may have many unfortunate consequences, such as limiting our genetic resources and ability to create new medicines and biochemicals. And ecosystems that are more biodiverse can sequester more CO_2 than can ecosystems with species-poor assemblages,[28] thus they help to decrease the likelihood of climate change. Also, many intricate connections exist between the physical environment and local, native organisms, as in the honey bee example mentioned earlier. Replacing the diverse array of natives with only a few exotics may have many unforeseen consequences, and doing so may be like placing all the eggs in one basket.

SOCIAL AND HEALTH BENEFITS

Whenever the pressure of our complex city life thins my blood and numbs my brain, I seek relief in the trail; and when I hear the coyote wailing to the yellow dawn, my cares fall from me—I am happy.
—Hamlin Garland, American novelist and poet

Natural areas help create a sense of place. Natural areas—forest areas, meadows, coral reefs, natural springs, rivers—contain a unique blend of plants, animals, and other organisms. Each location in the world has its own natural heritage, and people in all parts of the world are connected to the distinctive mix of plants, animals, geography, and climate in their area. Conservation and restoration of biodiversity in and around cities provide urban inhabitants with the opportunity to create a true sense of place. Valuable natural areas can be as small as an individual yard or a neighborhood pocket park. Creatively designed gardens and native landscaping can bring a bit of the natural environment right into urban surroundings, accommodating the needs of humans and wildlife. Natural areas within cities are often used to educate people about their environment and human history. A 2002 study found that when people are exposed to unstructured natural areas as children, they express more positive perceptions of natural environments and outdoor recreation activities later in life.[29] A number of studies have demonstrated that urban residents around the world desire contact with nature in an urban setting and have strong aesthetic preferences for community designs that incorporate natural areas.[30]

Interaction with natural areas promotes better human health. There is a growing body of evidence that our own psychological and physical well-being is rooted in our connection to nature.[31] Conversations about "biophilia" and "deep ecology" discuss the intricate link between nature and humans.[32] Even though many people live in urban environments, and most of their lives are spent in cars, homes, and other buildings, their emotional well-being and health depends on their ability to experience nature. The ways in which urban communities are built and maintained have direct and indirect consequences for natural environments and human health. People recover from stress more quickly when exposed to natural vegetation instead of urban settings.[33] It is especially important that children play outside. A 2003 *Environment and Behavior* article found that access to natural areas protects children from the impact of life stress.[34] Stress levels were reduced as kids spent more time playing outside, and this protective buffering intensifies with increasing stress levels within children. Furthermore, the amount of time spent in contact with nature affects a variety of human health factors, such as the level of cognitive functioning,[35] the number of physical ailments,[36] and the speed of recovery from illness.[37]

Natural areas provide shared green space for humans to interact and recreate. By incorporating green space and walkability into their designs, residential communities create areas where people can interact and recreate. Natural areas in cities promote interactions among residents[38] and recreation such as walking, playing, and watching wildlife in a more natural setting. One study found that a sense of place, attachment, and satisfaction were affected by not only social constructions but also the landscape attributes of the natural environment.[39] Conventional designs for cities, without walkable neighborhoods or green space, are counterproductive to an individual's need to experience community,[40] and urban residents really desire a sense of community.[41] In a review of *Landscape and Urban Planning* journal studies that looked at how humans interact with outdoor urban environments, the article found that people highly value natural urban areas in which to interact and play.[42]

Natural areas provide opportunities to watch wildlife. In urban areas, many people observe and interact with wildlife. People value watching wildlife, and surveys indicate that a vast amount of wildlife watching occurs in and around the home. Of a reported 71.1 million wildlife watchers in the United States, about 67.8 million people have observed wildlife around their homes.[43] Of these people who observe wildlife near their homes, 55.5 million reported feeding wildlife, 44.5 million observed wildlife, 18.8 million photographed wildlife, 14.5 million planted and maintained natural habitat, and 13.3 million people visited public parks to watch wildlife. Many public and private agencies have responded to this interest with programs about landscaping for wildlife and wildlife watching. The National Wildlife Federation (www.nwf.org), for example, has the Backyard Habitat Program, which provides tools and resources to help homeowners create wildlife habitat in their backyards, and several notable backyard bird surveys have been established online (e.g., Cornell Lab of Ornithology, www.birds.cornell.edu).

ECONOMIC BENEFITS

Healthy natural areas allow for tourism and recreation. Ecotourism provides a substantial income for many states. In the United States, hunting, fishing, and wildlife viewing generate approximately $122 billion in revenue. Of this, about $45.7 billion was spent on wildlife-watching activities alone, including equipment and travel expenditures.[44] And ecotourism is heavily influenced by the quality and quantity of developed areas. Unless sustainable development practices are implemented within a state, built areas ultimately affect the natural areas that tourists enjoy. In the United States, the tourism industry provides a substantial income for many state economies.

Preserved natural areas can increase property values. Most homeowners regard healthy natural open spaces located close to homes as aesthetically pleasing, and they value them.[45] In general, properties and homes located near urban natural areas have higher values. Two resource manuals on the economic value of green space can be found online:

1. *The Economic Benefits of Parks and Open Space*, published by the Trust for Public Land (www.tpl.org)
2. *Economic Impacts of Protecting Rivers, Trails, and Greenway Corridors: A Resource Book*, published by the National Park Service (www.nps.gov)

Preserving natural habitats can decrease irrigation costs. Native plants are adapted to an area's annual cycling of wet and dry seasons. By reducing the amount of formal landscaping that incorporates exotics, and preserving natural areas, developments can reduce or eliminate the need for irrigation.

Conserving open space can help to sell homes. A 2010 study indicates that homeowners living in both green communities and conventional ones want to have "green features" in their neighborhoods.[46] The features they asked for included open space, places to watch wildlife, and walkability. Furthermore, homes in conservation subdivisions tend to sell more quickly and at higher premiums.[47]

Established land use conservation options can provide direct cash payments or a substantial reduction in property rates. Options such as conservation easements, land donations, and land sales can preserve natural areas in perpetuity while providing economic incentives to land owners. Land is "sold" to a local land trust (see the Land Trust Alliance Web site, www.lta.org), and landowners receive money for taking land out of the realm of development. More details about conservation easements are discussed in chapter 3.

Some municipalities and organizations offer financial incentives to promote green building practices and natural resource conservation. Several municipalities offer quicker application reviews for developments that preserve natural areas or that are composed of energy-efficient homes. For example, the City of Gainesville, Florida, has a fast-track incentive and gives permit breaks to contractors who build energy-efficient homes.[48] Also, Fannie Mae offers a variety of incentives to homebuyers purchasing green homes.

'SUSTAINABLE DEVELOPMENT' AND 'GREEN COMMUNITY' DEFINED

Several definitions of *sustainability* and *sustainable development* can be found. A general one that captures the intention behind sustainable development was stated in 1987 by the United Nations World Commission on the Environment and Development: "Sustainable development is development that meets the needs of the present without compromising the ability of future generations to meet their own needs." This definition primarily refers to the development of an entire country. Addressing the basic needs of people in countries, while providing resources for both local and global markets, presents a set of problems and solutions that are related to, but different from, the way urban communities are built in countries like the United States. I use the terms *sustainable development, green development,* and *green community* interchangeably. Green communities feature several components, and I have highlighted three important ones:

1. Environmental integrity: green communities conserve natural resources and minimize impacts.

2. Sense of community: people in green communities are connected with their neighbors.

TABLE 2   EXAMPLES OF GREEN DEVELOPMENTS THAT HAVE AN
ECOLOGICAL FOCUS

Green Developments and Organizations with Examples of Green Developments	Web Sites
Madera, Florida	www.wec.ufl.edu/extension/gc/madera/
Town of Harmony, Florida	www.harmonyfl.com/lih/index.htm
Prairie Crossing, Illinois	www.prairiecrossing.com
The Woodlands at Davidson, North Carolina	www.thewoodlandsatdavidson.com
Earthsong, New Zealand	www.earthsong.org.nz
Global Ecovillage Network	http://gen.ecovillage.org
Sustainable Sites Initiative	www.sustainablesites.org
New Zealand communities	http://cs.synergine.com

3. Health: the homes, yards, and neighborhoods have a positive impact on
   our psychological and physical health.

Some may quibble about the importance of these three principles, and each
person may feel most strongly about one or two of these principles. Yet all of
these components are interconnected in many direct and indirect ways. For
instance, the conservation of urban natural areas can also mean the conservation of local biodiversity, as well as provide places for people to interact with
each other and improve their psychological and physical health.[49] In this book,
I give ideas that directly address the issue of environmental integrity. Whenever I use the term *green community* or *sustainable development*, I am thinking
about all three components as they are interrelated, but I explicitly concentrate
on methodologies to conserve biodiversity. As mentioned previously, conserving biodiversity can promote a sense of community, a healthy environment,
and even economic vitality.

Around the world, a sustainable movement is under way, and a few green
development initiatives have popped up (Table 2). Each green community
project is different, and each varies in its degree of emphasis on biodiversity conservation. From my experience, most green communities emphasize
energy-efficient housing and walkable communities, and place only a minor
emphasis on biodiversity. In recent years, the term *conservation subdivisions* has
been used in the landscape architecture, planning, and environmental community to get across the concept of satisfying habitat needs for both humans
and wildlife.[50] The concept of a conservation subdivision is to group houses
together on smaller lots, with the remaining areas left as open space. Seen as

an alternative to conventional designs, conservation subdivisions have been promoted as a benefit to wildlife and a way to enhance an area's rural character.[51] The concept of conservation subdivision is popular in the planning and design fields, especially in new urbanist literature, and is regarded as a design methodology to create more natural communities.[52] Clustering homes to conserve open space is a step in the right direction, but many other aspects of design and management must be considered if we are to create functional habitat that supports a diversity of species. Simply conserving a percentage of open space may not be enough to conserve biodiversity, because many other ecological, environmental, and management issues come into play.[53]

CHAPTER 2

Urban Decision Makers

A cross-section of society (residents, developers, policy makers) makes decisions that interact in specific ways to affect natural resources. Usually, growth management conflicts are win-lose; on one side developers want to develop a piece of land with very few restrictions, and on the other side environmentalists want to stop the development. These conflicting entities end up in court, and one side wins and the other side loses. But a middle ground is achievable, and communities can grow and strive to reduce their negative impacts on biodiversity.

The "greenness" of communities is the result of collective decisions made by residents, developers, and policy makers; each stakeholder plays a role in creating a green community. Residents constitute one decision level, one that includes both people who rent and those who own property. The developer level includes not only the developer but also the other built environment professionals who help shape a proposed development, such as landscape architects, architects, contractors, civil engineers, and real estate agents. The developer typically hires these individuals, and they have considerable influence on the final development plan. The policy-maker level includes governmental staff such as policy makers and regulators, who develop policies, review development proposals, and make recommendations about future growth strategies. Also included in this group are elected government officials who have the final say about submitted land use changes, growth management plans, and proposed policies.

Decisions at the three stakeholder levels are hierarchical in the sense that upper-level decisions constrain lower-level decisions. At the policy-maker level, governments create land use plans and maps—called comprehensive

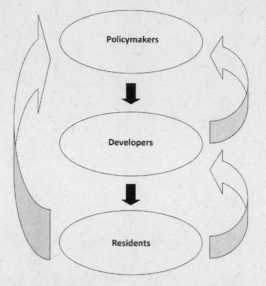

FIGURE 1. Policy makers constrain the decisions made by developers, and developers constrain the decisions of residents. Residents, though, because of voting and purchasing power, can influence the decisions made by developers and policy makers. In addition, developers wielding economic power can dramatically influence policy depending on local political conditions.

development plans in some states, such as Florida—and these plans are designed to manage growth by encouraging or regulating where growth can occur. Within a jurisdiction, lands are given a specific land use category, such as single-family residential or agriculture. For a given land use, county or city policy makers craft land development regulations, which dictate how the land will be developed. Thus, decisions by policy makers constrain where a developer can build a subdivision and how the development will look. Developers, in turn, create the *framework* for the subdivision, which encompasses everything from the layout of the entire site to the details of how individual homes are to be built. This framework ultimately constrains what a resident can or cannot do, as it would be difficult to change what a developer has put in place. However, at the resident level, people must manage their homes, yards, and neighborhoods in a way that does not compromise the original intent of the community.

At each decision level, design and management decisions are critical in the creation of a biodiverse community. Each decision influences the others: the decisions made by policy makers influence the decisions made by developers; developers affect the decisions made by residents; and residents are influenced by decisions made by policy makers and developers. There is a feedback loop, though: residents, through their purchasing and voting power, can influence developers and policy makers. Also developers, using their economic muscle, can influence policy makers (Figure 1). Decisions to adopt biodiversity-conservation practices are not only based on the current understanding of sustainable practices and technologies but are also related to a number of socioeconomic, political, and even personal factors. It will be useful to explore in more detail the roles of policy makers, developers, and residents in creating green communities.

COUNTY AND CITY POLICY MAKERS

At the planning level, decisions made by county and city planning staff and elected officials create plans for how a community will grow for a number of years (Figure 2). Growth management plans form the basis for the way a community regulates development and how it invests in services and infrastructure. These municipal master plans, sometimes called comprehensive development plans, regulate where and how land can be subdivided. Plans and policies set forth by governments affect the design and management of a community at broad and local scales. Although somewhat constrained by state and national policies, decisions at the local level usually have the most influence. Local government decisions constrain or promote the sustainability of a community, ultimately affecting the ability of critters and plants to survive in and around cities. For instance, lands within a jurisdiction could be evaluated for their conservation value, and different parcels would be marked for development and others slated for conservation. A variety of policy initiatives could be implemented to conserve the most significant lands (e.g., a public referendum to generate monies to purchase land), and growth plans could tightly regulate developed areas in order to minimize the impact of daily human activities on nearby natural areas. In addition, regulations could stipulate that developments near protected areas would have decreased housing densities. Habitats for endangered and threatened species could be identified and conserved through a number of different regulatory and incentive-based policies. It is tricky to balance public perception and values, socioeconomic and environmental concerns, and of course, politics. All these factors determine which policies affecting land use are implemented and enforced across a community.

FIGURE 2. County or city planners, with some input from the public, develop growth management plans to regulate how a community grows. Sometimes called comprehensive development plans, they include a future land use map designating specific uses of the land, such as agriculture or residential use. Each land use has land development regulations associated with it, and these offer general and specific designations about the type of development that can occur there. Governments ultimately adopt these plans, and elected officials approve any changes to them. Such planning directs where and how developers can subdivide land. Drawing by Meryl Klein.

Policy and planning considerations set the stage for "smart growth." Across a region, smart-growth policies help to determine where growth occurs, and such plans can conserve large natural areas that promote biodiversity. In addition, small but significant patches of natural habitat are often embedded in urban and rural land, and deserve protection. For instance, a large subdivision may contain within its boundaries significant natural areas worthy of conserving in order to enhance urban biodiversity and minimize impacts on natural lands that are adjacent to the property. As mentioned earlier, protected pieces of land are affected by what happens in built and agricultural areas. How urban and rural lands are designed and *managed*, over the long term, determines whether a city or county conserves biodiversity across a region.

Once a parcel is designated for development, land development regulations (LDRs) restrict what a developer can do. The particulars of these regulations are derived from the comprehensive development plan and contain such elements as zoning maps, subdivision regulations, infrastructure design standards, and public facility requirements. Considering biodiversity conservation, LDRs could stipulate design and management practices that promote biodiversity.

Examples include the use of native plants in landscaped areas, clustering of homes to protect significant natural areas, and use of water-efficient irrigation technologies. In some instances, current LDRs may actually prevent the adoption of sustainable practices, because regulators may not understand and give credit for the use of new practices. As an example, rain gardens and swales, which are designed to capture stormwater, may not be recognized as practices that meet stormwater regulations. Instead of permitting rain gardens and swales, regulators may choose to stick with conventional practices, which utilize curbs, culverts, and pipes that transport water directly to retention ponds.

Policies, land use plans, LDRs, the allocation of funds, and even public education efforts by city and county agencies, greatly influence how well biodiversity conservation works. Public engagement is particularly important because individual decisions in neighborhoods can affect natural areas. One detrimental decision that homeowners may make is to unknowingly plant and maintain invasive exotic plant species. Invasive exotic plants are introduced plants known to take over and significantly alter natural habitats. Governments that support educational efforts to prevent and eradicate invasive exotics in built areas will help to prevent the spread of invasives into nearby natural areas. Even bicycle paths and pedestrian walkways in and around conserved natural areas must be maintained and regulated over a number of years. People and pets running through natural areas can destroy important plant and animal communities. Without policies that encourage a good education and management plan (and funding to back it up!), even the best design intentions may fail.

Because policies that affect growth operate across a range of scales, they can constrain the effectiveness of sustainable decisions made by developers and residents. If a developer wants to implement sustainable options, how can he or she do this if a practice is not permitted by current regulations? Clustering homes, for example, may not be permitted under current LDRs. A developer may not be able to use swales and rain gardens for stormwater management because the curb-and-gutter method may be the only one recognized by city regulatory policies. And if homeowners want to let their lawn grass grow out to a more natural state, how can they do so if strict city ordinances regulate how tall grass can grow? Some policies created in an earlier era are outdated and should be removed or updated to promote creativity and the ability to implement conservation practices. Well-intentioned developers or residents should not have their hands tied when trying to implement a particular design or management strategy that improves biodiversity measures.

Across a city or county, policy makers must look at the big picture and help developers and residents implement their ideas in a way that makes the entire community sustainable. For example, several well-intentioned developers may want to conserve 50 percent of their developments as open space. However, they may not think beyond the boundaries of their own developments, and if thirty different developments conserve open space but do not coordinate and plan for connectivity, a real opportunity is lost. *Connectivity* refers to the connection of trail systems to promote the movement of people between communities; it also can enhance the movement of wildlife across the landscape. Unfortunately, a 2009 study indicated that, across several cities, planning department personnel spent little time on biodiversity conservation issues.[1]

Where comprehensive planning occurs, it is important to place the master plan first when considering rezoning and variances. In his book *Ecologically Based Municipal Land Use Planning*,[2] William Honachefsky points out that many zoning laws are changed haphazardly with little regard to a comprehensive development plan. He argues further that smart planning is achieved not by adding more regulations and laws but through community involvement in land use planning. Also, a priority for the master plan must be to conserve an area's ecological infrastructure. Although some communities are beginning to see the natural, social, and cultural values of land, many of the best attempts to produce meaningful, comprehensive development plans are compromised by the ease with which these plans can be changed to accommodate various economic interests. As an example, the bellwether state of Florida passed the Growth Management Act of 1985, with its novel requirement for comprehensive development plans. This act did set forth a requirement stating that every county must develop a comprehensive development plan. Unfortunately, these plans were often not followed, or annual variances to the plans were allowed in response to the whim of political and economic forces. Some Floridians grew despondent about growth management, and a growth management amendment was placed on the ballot in 2010, although it did not pass. Called the Hometown Democracy Amendment, this amendment represents an additional step in growth management.[3] Essentially, once elected officials approve the amendment of a local comprehensive development plan, this plan change is put to a public vote. Thus, any major changes to a master plan will be passed only after public approval. This amendment is similar to one passed in Escondido, California, the Escondido Growth Management and Neighborhood Protection Act, commonly referred to as Proposition S.

The message is that policy makers and regulators must be on the same page to create and support good growth management policies. The public, in turn, must elect and provide support for political leaders who explicitly strive to create meaningful biodiversity policies. The policies and growth management plans developed by municipalities are critical factors in creating a culture of sustainability. In essence, governments create the conditions that enable communities to adopt practices that conserve biodiversity in and around cities. When land is designated for subdividing, good planning regulations insure that biodiversity conservation is a priority, and that newly created subdivisions not only conserve biodiversity on-site but also have minimal impact on surrounding environments.

DEVELOPERS AND BUILT ENVIRONMENT PROFESSIONALS

Even with good growth management policies, it is really up to developers to follow the intent of policies and to make good decisions during the development process (Figure 3). There is often plenty of wiggle room for developers to implement their own ideas, despite being directed by LDRs. With the stroke of a pen, a developer sets the tone for the community for decades to come. Such decisions create community infrastructure that is difficult to change—lot sizes, landscape palettes, transportation routes, and housing stock. If all yards are dominated by turfgrass, and the perceived social norm of the neighborhood is mowed turfgrass, it would be difficult to convert a front lawn to native vegetation. Also, the developer may have placed covenants on the property that dictate a high percentage of the front yard must be turf. A determined individual could buck the system, but individual stewards may not transform the community if the community does not support such actions and deed restrictions prevent them.

The way a developer sets up a community is important, because the collective impact of maintaining yards and homes on the environment is large. Initial decisions by developers and their development teams shape the way homes and yards will be maintained far into the future. Cumulatively, individual homes and yards consume vast amounts of energy and water and have the potential of negatively affecting the environment. People take showers, heat and cool their homes, and water and fertilize their yards; the initial designs installed by the developer affect the efficiency of homes and yards. If a developer-chosen landscape palette consists of primarily exotic and *invasive*

FIGURE 3. Developers, under the constraints of current planning guidelines and negotiations, determine the essential framework of a community. They decide where the roads go, how big the lots and homes are, how many homes to build, the type of landscaping to install, how much impervious surface to construct, whether to conserve open space, and so on. Such decisions essentially determine how the community will look, feel, and function over many years to come. It would be difficult for residents to change the look and feel of the community once it has been constructed. Drawing by Meryl Klein.

plants, it can be detrimental, because exotics typically require extra water, fertilizers, and pesticides to help them flourish, and the invasive plant species have a way of escaping and affecting nearby natural areas (e.g., Chinese tallow trees, *Sapium sebiferum*, used in the Southeast, have spread into natural areas). Even the choice of stormwater treatment trains and impervious surfaces can result in excess pollutants being carried off-site, affecting biodiversity in nearby wetlands, rivers, and lakes. Also, the way homes are built dictates energy consumption, and energy consumption ultimately entails the conversion of natural areas (e.g., hilltops are blasted in order to mine coal), and drilling for oil in sensitive environments (e.g., offshore drilling in deep water).

Developer decisions are sculpted by cultural, economic, and personal tastes. A development's design is critical to the long-term conservation of natural resources. A good overall development plan will have appropriate site layouts and building designs, as well as management and educational plans that encourage residents to participate in natural resource conservation. After all, once the developer leaves, it is up to each person in a neighborhood to maintain and even create conservation strategies appropriate to the larger community. So developers play a significant role in ensuring that biodiversity conservation continues over the long term.

FIGURE 4. Two homeowners in the arid southwestern United States. The one on the left maintains a lawn in the middle of a desert ecosystem. The one on the right has installed a more biodiverse yard with native plants, gravel, and no turfgrass. Such individual decisions are shaped by values, city and neighborhood regulations, social norms, and past experiences. If all the homeowners in a neighborhood planted primarily turfgrass on their lots, the consumption of water and fertilizers would be much greater than in a neighborhood with native landscaping. Drawing by Meryl Klein.

RESIDENTS

Never doubt that a small group of thoughtful, committed citizens can change the world; indeed, it's the only thing that ever has.

—Margaret Mead

Within limitations set forth by policy makers and developers, residents make day-to-day decisions that determine the look and feel of any neighborhood and town (Figure 4). Each rental or owned property is ultimately governed by the decisions made by people living on the property. Driving through a hypothetical subdivision, one might see manicured, green lawns occupying a majority of the front yards, landscaped areas with ornamental flowers and shrubs, sprinklers running during the middle of the day, and large amounts of bagged leaves and grass clippings stacked on the curb for pick up. Alternatively, one might see properties that have little lawn in front, lots of native trees and shrubs, a few snags (dead trees), highly efficient micro-irrigation systems, and neatly tucked-away compost bins that convert most of the yard debris into soil. These two scenarios certainly give different impressions. Each action, although constrained by what the developer initially installed, was molded and shaped by individual values, societal norms, and the influence of neighbors right next door. If a majority of homeowners choose to landscape their yards with native plants, this becomes the community norm, and native plants become a familiar choice and preference. In neighborhoods that lack environmental stewardship, a few local champions can go a long way to augment peoples' knowledge and shift their attitudes and behaviors. Even one enterprising homeowner could educate others about state-of-the-art conservation strategies for the home, yard, and shared spaces throughout the neighborhood. Such local stewards can be a significant voice in the neighborhood, helping to spread conservation principles and practices.

Supported by local policies and plans, a developer may have implemented a good conservation design, but this plan can go astray if residents do not understand or want to conserve biodiversity. Yards, homes, and shared open spaces require management over time, and individuals may make decisions that are not conducive to biodiversity conservation. Native landscapes could be replaced with turfgrass, improper applications of fertilizers and pesticides would affect natural areas, the installation of invasive exotic plants would result in invasives taking over natural areas, and the decision to allow pets to roam outdoors would disturb wildlife populations. Informed residents who have expressed a community-wide goal to create a resource-efficient, healthy community may help to conserve local biodiversity and wildlife species of concern, but other residents may resort to conventional, nonenvironmental behaviors. A study in Florida found that residents of a supposedly green community scored lower on several questions about environmental knowledge, attitudes, and behavior than people in conventional communities.[4] Just because a green subdivision was built correctly, this does not necessarily mean that the community will function as a community that conserves biodiversity.

Understanding biodiversity conservation is one factor, but it is critical that residents also have a sense of community. Connection with neighbors can help establish a neighborhood social norm and promote the idea of managing homes, yards, and neighborhoods in an environmentally sensitive way. Social norms have been shown to have a strong influence on motivating behavior, and this could work strongly for or against environmental conservation.[5] In some studies, results have indicated that obvious social norms were better predictors of recycling than environmental attitudes.[6] Sense of community is important for the dispersal of social norms concerning attitudes, knowledge, and behaviors relevant to the environment. Loss of community can result in a loss of empowerment, and empowerment, too, may be important for motivating environmentally friendly behaviors.[7] Many sociologists believe that a sense of community has been declining for several decades in the United States.[8] People today are less likely to know and interact with their neighbors than they were in past generations.[9] This loss of a perceived sense of community may be affecting biodiversity conservation goals, because the social diffusion of environmental knowledge and conservation behaviors may be inhibited.

URBAN AREAS ARE KEY!

To summarize part 1, the design and management of urban environments are critical to the future of biodiversity conservation. No longer can urban environments be discounted and efforts focused primarily on natural areas outside of cities. The urban-wildland interface is expanding, and impacts stemming from urban areas are occurring farther and farther away from the source. Not all of what occurs within the boundaries of a city stays within its boundaries, and special care is needed to design and manage neighborhoods in ways that promote biodiversity within municipal boundaries as well as help minimize impacts on surrounding natural areas. Many biodiversity-conservation impacts have originated in urban centers: pollution of freshwaters and oceans, invasive plants and animals in natural areas, and habitat destruction and fragmentation. The consumption of food, energy, and other natural resources is a driving factor that will ultimately determine how degraded natural ecosystems will become. With billions of people living in urban areas, a unique opportunity exists to provide opportunities for people to understand and connect with their natural heritage. Urban biodiversity experiences are an important factor in developing a conservation ethic; ultimately they affect the ability of public and private conservation organizations to further their missions. Scientists around the world recognize the need to address urban biodiversity conservation (see Box 1), and the task at hand is to address environmental, social, and economic issues together in order for biodiverse communities to be realized.

Conserving urban biodiversity makes environmental, social, and economic sense. Ecosystems annually provide billions of dollars' worth of services, and their long-term health is directly and indirectly related to the decisions made by individuals who live, work, and play in urban centers. The ability of nearby wetlands to purify and remove contaminants from water is related to the amount of pollutants carried in stormwater discharge. Biodiverse communities help to create a sense of place and have many other social and health benefits, such as enabling people to recover from stress and illness. People value urban natural areas for recreation, interaction, and the opportunity to experience nature. Millions of people watch wildlife in their backyards and urban parks. And planning for biodiversity conservation helps homeowners economically through increased property values and decreased landscape management requirements; it helps developers by increasing house premiums and sales; and it ultimately improves ecotourism by making healthy ecosystems available for tourists to enjoy.

When a variety of stakeholders have a vested interest in urban biodiversity conservation, one might expect that it would be relatively easy to alter conventional development practices. However, one must not underestimate the power of inertia, societal norms, and the perception that protecting the environment translates into economic losses. And yet, while these are huge hurdles to overcome, model communities that conserve biodiversity present local examples from which other people can gain insight and a level of comfort that lets them strike out on their own. To create the first well-designed and managed subdivision requires the involvement of the public, developers, the built environment community, and policy makers. Leaving out even one of these stakeholders will most likely result in a dysfunctional subdivision, or a development project that never gets off the ground. Policy makers establish the enabling conditions that promote the uptake of good design and management practices that promote biodiversity. Engaged developers who understand biodiversity conservation help to insure that the best designs and management practices are implemented on a site. An engaged public facilitates the long-term management of conservation subdivisions and creates a demand for such construction practices.

PART TWO

The Devil Is in the Details

Keep on going and the chances are you will stumble on something, perhaps when you are least expecting it. I have never heard of anyone stumbling on something sitting down.
—Charles F. Kettering, American inventor

I don't know the key to success, but the key to failure is to try to please everyone.
—Bill Cosby

Incorporating biodiversity conservation into the design and management of residential communities is a tall order and is often plagued with uncertainties and unknowns. As discussed earlier in the book, community biodiversity conservation can be maximized through environmentally sensitive development techniques, and it provides economic and social benefits. In the United States, the public is very interested in green development, as indicated by the hundreds of state ballot initiatives that have been proposed.[1] Researchers are beginning to measure the positive (and negative) impacts of green communities.[2] In the end, the creation and maintenance of a functioning green community is shaping up to be a paradigm shift in the building and construction community. Conventional-development inertia is a strong force, but examples of developments that incorporate biodiversity design and management principles can be found in some communities. Many green designs and management practices are based on scientific principles and research; some of these designs and practices have been tried, but many are yet to be wholly adopted for biodiversity conservation. People may balk at the risk of attempting something new, but advances in the art of creating green communities depend on thoughtful consideration and on somebody taking the first leap. In the end, each green community built will help facilitate the creation of additional green communities, as these working models make it progressively easier for developers to attempt something different and for cities to encourage new designs and management methods that promote biodiversity.

Before I discuss in detail the specific issues and practices that can improve biodiversity when land is subdivided, it is important to understand the three phases of a development: *design, construction,* and *postconstruction* (Figure 5). Each phase is critical and must be addressed if a site is to conserve biodiversity over the long term. During the design phase, a developer will confer with a variety of professional environmental consultants, who will give advice and make design recommendations for the subdivision to help get it approved by the county or city government. The consulting team—composed of civil engineers, architects, surveyors, landscape architects, and other professionals—will review existing regulations and present a site plan to the local planning board. At this stage, everything is laid out on paper, and the discussion is about where things go and the juxtaposition of vertical structures (i.e., buildings) and horizontal structures (i.e., roads, lots, and shared spaces). Once a project is demonstrated to be in compliance with local regulations, the project is permitted. Next is the construction phase: here, a host of contractors and subcontractors implements the plan, constructing homes, streets, utility lines, and landscaped areas. Large earthwork machines are used to sculpt the earth according to the initial design. Typically, the landscaping palette (e.g., natives or exotic plants and the amount of turf) is finalized at this stage. As lots are built, landscapes are filled in with a selection of plants and turf. After homes are built and sold, people move into the community and manage their own homes, yards, and neighborhood.

The design phase is important because it is the framework that defines the community for decades to come. After roads, buildings, and conserved natural areas are created, it would be difficult to change their locations. For example, once large trees are removed and significant natural areas are bulldozed, it would take a long time to grow new trees and impossible to restore significant natural areas if buildings, turf, and pavement occupy these areas. Even the way homes are distributed among wetlands and significant uplands can make or break the biodiversity value of a property. If built areas surround a distribution of small, isolated patches of natural habitat, this highly fragmented site will not conserve local sensitive animal and plant species.

While design is important, over the long term the construction and postconstruction phases potentially have the most impact on biodiversity.[3] Without trained or fully engaged contractors or landscapers, many things can happen

(a)

FIGURE 5. The three phases of a development are design, construction, and postconstruction. In the design phase, built areas—that is, homes and roads—and conserved open spaces, if any, are designated and formally drawn on paper. This master plan (a) is a guide to where construction will take place. In the construction phase, the plan is implemented. Here, earthwork machines move soil around to lay down the foundations for roads, homes, and utilities (b, next page). In the postconstruction phase, people move into the community (c, next page). It is now up to the homeowners to manage their homes, yards, and neighborhoods far into the future. Courtesy of Harmony Development Co., Jeanette Hostetler, and Steve Allen.

during the construction phase that affect the viability of future natural resource conservation. For instance, even if the most important large trees are preserved across the subdivision, and built areas are designed around them, the placement of fill dirt and the routes for heavy construction vehicles are critical to the survival of these trees. It's not enough to place a fence or flagging around the trunk

(b)

(c)

of a tree. A sturdy fence must protect the roots that lie within the drip line (the outer edge of the leafy canopy). If heavy vehicles continually run over the root zone of a tree, or fill dirt is placed right up to the tree trunk, the roots may not be able to acquire nutrients, water, and oxygen, and the tree may die. Further, once the homes are built and people move into a neighborhood, additional problems can arise if residents are not fully engaged. Cats and dogs allowed to run about the various conserved natural areas would cause havoc with the local wildlife. Thus, sustainable development is a function of both *design* and *management*. It is essential that the creators of urban designs adopt a vision of "design over time," a perspective that recognizes that urban landscapes change over time, and that long-term management is an evolving process.[4]

I have organized part 2 of this book into eight chapters that are related to biodiversity conservation and restoration in subdivision development. In each chapter, I give some background about a few specific issues, review case studies and working examples, and suggest specific conservation actions. As discussed earlier, policy makers, developers, and residents all make decisions that affect the ability of developments to conserve biodiversity. These stakeholders have an effect on the design, construction, and postconstruction phases of subdivision development. For example, policy makers can pass a variety of ordinances that directly affect what goes on during the design, construction, and postconstruction phases, influencing the decisions of both developers and homeowners.

Therefore, in each chapter I divide the discussion into three sections: What Can Residents in a Neighborhood Do? What Can a Developer Do? and What Can a Policy Maker Do? Residents are people who actually live in a subdivision, either owning or renting places in which to live. Developers are built environment professionals who subdivide land; others in this group include hired environmental consultants, contractors, and large or small landowners. Policy makers include elected officials, planning staff, and various public agencies who regulate growth. In each section, I highlight specific actions that a policy maker, developer, or resident could undertake to conserve biodiversity in a master-planned development.

CHAPTER 3

Tree Protection and Natural Area Preservation Strategies

Natural areas, even single trees, found on a site are valuable resources; conserving them enhances biodiversity and is part of the larger effort to conserve natural resources. If topsoil is scraped away and large trees are chopped down, it sometimes takes hundreds to thousands of years to reestablish the same collection of species. In particular, the soil on a site is full of soil biota, including thousands of beneficial bacteria, worms, and fungi. If the soil has not previously been disturbed, it is also an excellent source of local seeds. Preserving local topsoil and above ground vegetation will conserve animals and plants already found on the property. This critical step, conserving what is already there, is key, because it is difficult to restore a piece of land once destroyed. Conserving trees and natural patches of ground is essential to the long-term goal of conserving biodiversity.

Native trees in urban areas enhance biodiversity simply because an assortment of native trees retained on a site will conserve the local diversity; these trees also provide habitat for other native plants and animals. They also provide many valuable ecosystem services; for example, they reduce the stormwater flow by intercepting a portion of the rain as it hits the trees' leaves, branches, and trunks. This can be a significant savings. In the metropolitan Washington, D.C., region, the city's existing 46 percent tree canopy cover reduces the need for stormwater-retention structures by 949 million cubic feet, and is valued at $4.7 billion per twenty-year construction cycle (based on a five-dollar-per-cubic-foot construction cost).[1] Trees also benefit air quality, because they remove many pollutants from the atmosphere, including nitrogen dioxide, sulfur dioxide, ozone, and carbon monoxide. Tree cover reduces energy costs significantly by shading homes; the organization American Forests found that tree cover in the Atlanta area saved residents approximately $2.8 million annually in reduced energy costs.[2]

Urban natural areas serve as habitat for local plants and animals, but local residents enjoy these urban natural areas too. In 1995, American LIVES, a San Francisco–based marketing and research firm, conducted a survey on what American homebuyers desire in new residential developments.[3] Their findings showed the growing importance of natural areas. "Lots of natural, open space" and an abundance of "walking and biking paths" were respectively listed as the number two and three most important features for new homebuyers, behind "neighborhood designs featuring quiet and low traffic flows." Wilderness areas that harbor plants and animals native to a neighborhood's predeveloped parcel of land were also listed as valuable amenities. The effective integration of preserved natural communities, human-made nature parks and trails, and social interaction in what American LIVES termed the new "outdoor living room" can bring additional profits to a development venture while simultaneously conserving biodiversity.

If natural areas are selected and managed well, they can provide important wildlife habitat that will increase local biodiversity and provide ample wildlife viewing opportunities for residents to enjoy. Each animal has particular habitat requirements, but if these are taken into account, a variety of species can reside within urban areas.[4] However, one must be careful, as wildlife-human conflicts can increase. Urban wildlife problems ultimately stem from human behavior, because wildlife species "do what they do" naturally and respond to the actions of humans. Animals are labeled as a nuisance because people become less tolerant of a species, or because humans intentionally or unintentionally create a resource that animals exploit. A few notable wildlife species have reached large numbers in urban areas and are often considered a nuisance. Examples include raccoons and bears getting into garbage cans, squirrels living and raising their young in houses, deer eating landscaped plants, armadillos digging in lawns and gardens, and flocks of birds leaving droppings that soil buildings, pavements, and water retention ponds. An analysis of a national wildlife damage database maintained by USDA-APHIS Wildlife Services, shows that, from 1994 through 2003, economic damage from urban wildlife reached about $550.8 million.[5] However, most conflicts can be avoided.

Residents, developers, and policy makers play important roles in providing wildlife habitat while, at the same time, minimizing wildlife-human conflicts.

WHAT CAN RESIDENTS IN A NEIGHBORHOOD DO?

If a neighborhood has an assortment of preserved trees and natural areas, it is up to residents and others to properly maintain and protect these areas. Care must be taken with activities in and around natural areas. Human activities near the edges of these areas can disturb wildlife and disrupt the growth of native vegetation. If trails are located in natural areas, it is imperative that people and pets stay on these trails and do not wander into the natural areas. The regular trampling of vegetation can provide a pathway for exotics to become established, and human noise alone will disturb nesting and foraging animals.[6]

Often, though, it is difficult to engage the entire neighborhood in the proper maintenance of conserved areas. One option is to form a conservation club that meets fairly regularly to involve people in conservation management. For example, in Springvale, Maine, the Mousam Lake Region Association was formed with the primary purpose of cleaning up Mousam Lake (Box 2). Other ideas to promote environmental stewardship are: establish a regular newsletter; organize neighborhood environmental events such as cleanups and the removal of invasive exotic plants; promote an award for the neighborhood conservationist of the year; and conduct environmental activities with local school children. Wildlife found in urban areas should be treated with respect, and each resident should be aware of the dangers of feeding wildlife. Even the best intentions can create human-wildlife conflicts that would be difficult to resolve—for example, feeding raccoons only makes them tame and bold, and such animals become a nuisance in a neighborhood.

Elected officials govern most planning decisions, and the public can vote for officials who have a keen interest in sustainability and biodiversity conservation. I am reluctant to discuss politics here, but in terms of preserving natural habitat within a county, good policy makers can really promote a township's stewardship. Often, actions at the government level dictate how growth will occur over decades to come and how the environment will be managed in established neighborhoods. In Las Vegas, Nevada, local policies have encouraged homeowners to remove water-thirsty lawns and replace them with desert landscaping. The Southern Nevada Water Authority essentially pays homeowners $1.00–$1.50 per square foot of grass that is replaced with desert landscaping (www.snwa.com/html/cons_wsl.html). Similarly, the Arizona Municipal Water Users Association offers a variety of rebates to those who conserve water and install desert landscaping in certain municipalities in Arizona (www.amwua.org/rebates.html). These landscaping policies help with the management of conserved natural areas, because managing landscaped yards can produce pollutants that end up in nearby natural areas (see chapter 5). Plus, public policy can help to encourage developers to build compact developments that conserve natural open space. But even good policies must have teeth in them, which means that they do not bend at the whims of economic and political forces. Whether such policies stay in place over the long term depends on public support throughout a county (i.e., voters must get out and vote for the appropriate leadership). Developers often have much more

---

Box 2. Restoration of Mousam Lake

The shoreline of Mousam Lake, located in southern Maine, is lined by more than seasonal and year-round homes. Starting in the late 1970s, people noticed the decline of the lake's water quality. The main cause was the conversion of forested land to development, which resulted in increased runoff from roads and lawns and leaking septic tank systems. Phosphorous in the stormwater led to excessive algal growth and to decreases in water clarity and dissolved oxygen. In 1998, the state added Mousam Lake to the state's list of impaired water bodies.

Assessment of the lake showed that that the annual phosphate loading of 556 kg/yr would have to be reduced by 27 percent, to 150 kg/yr. To help manage this natural lake and its shoreline, the Mousam Lake Region Association was formed (http://mousamlake.org/aboutus.html). Residents from around the lake initiated a number of practices and activities to help save the lake. In partnership, local municipalities, homeowners, and the Environmental Protection Agency implemented erosion control practices around the lake. These practices included the planting of swales on developed properties, septic tank repair, and improved soil stabilization along gravel roads (Figure 6). A successful citizen education campaign was implemented—a series of events called Septic Socials, where people gathered to discuss best management practices. As a result of these efforts over a ten-year period, the lake's water became clear one meter deeper than it had been during the period of least clarity in the 1990s. The Maine Department of Environmental Protection has removed Mousam Lake from its list of impaired water bodies.

Source: U.S. Environmental Protection Agency. "Section 319, Nonpoint Source Program Success Story—Maine," 2008, www.epa.gov/owow/nps/Success319/state/me_mousam.htm.

staying power and resources than environmentalists and other concerned citizens during debates and the formation of growth management policies and plans. Elected officials with an understanding of biodiversity conservation are critical in the effort to make sure that the intent of environmental policies is followed when growth management issues arise.

I suggest getting involved in local politics and attending meetings of the board of commissioners when growth management issues are discussed or when there is a petition for a land use change. I cannot stress enough how important it is for green politicians to have the support of their constituents. When sustainability becomes a part of a government's and a town's culture, then the conservation of natural areas has a good chance to be realized within a local community.

Figure 6. Local residents plant native vegetation along the shore of Mousam Lake, Maine. Photo by Wendy Garland.

WHAT CAN A DEVELOPER DO?

A developer's first priority should be to conserve what is already present, even the one or two native tree species found on a site. Every location has unique natural areas and plants that could be conserved for biodiversity. Specific inventories that identify important plants and animals should be conducted to first pinpoint the areas of highest conservation value. However, a good design that identifies significant natural areas to be conserved must be accompanied by a good construction site management plan. Even the best site design can be destroyed during the construction phase, because inappropriate construction practices may occur, such as when workers drive heavy earthwork machines over the root zones of conserved trees. Postconstruction issues, such as how residents behave in and around conserved areas, will affect the biological integrity of the site over the long term. Concerning tree protection and natural-area preservation strategies, developers can significantly affect what goes on during the design, construction, and postconstruction phases. Each phase has its own nuances, and although all the phases are interrelated, I break up the discussion here and highlight important practices and concepts for each phase.

Design Phase

Analyze Significant Natural Resources

Preservation of the most significant natural resources on developed property depends on a thorough natural resource inventory.[7] This requires the coordination of experts from a variety of disciplines. The following surveys are useful when planning to conserve significant trees and natural areas:

- Vegetation and tree survey
- Topographical and soil survey
- Hydrologic survey
- Wildlife survey
- Wetland survey

The results of these surveys will enable a developer to prioritize the conservation of significant open space and determine the placement of roads and built areas. The designation of built and natural areas is a balance of economic and natural factors, and with a little thought a developer can conserve highly valued natural areas while providing the built infrastructure and homes to make a profit.

Focus Development on Previously Disturbed Sites

The areas with the most biodiversity—which are the most valuable to conserve—are usually the more pristine areas. Degraded areas typically contain exotic plants and may have had a recent human use (e.g., pastureland) that contributed to their loss of biodiversity. Site disturbances range from forestry management practices, grazing, and agricultural uses to the more permanent and disruptive urban uses. It is best to build in areas already altered by buildings and roads or other human uses. Concentrating development on agricultural areas, for example, will help conserved forested areas (Box 3). In drawing up construction plans, it is desirable to preserve most landform features, such as old sand dunes, cypress domes, and dry river beds, rather than building on them. In essence, existing topography and natural landforms should be respected; developers should not try to reengineer the small mounds, depressions, and other minute topographic relief. As stated earlier, the first step is to preserve what already exists, because it is difficult to later restore.

Box 3. Building in Agricultural Areas: Harmony, Florida

The town of Harmony is located just outside St. Cloud along Highway 192 in Osceola County, Florida. This new eleven-thousand-acre mixed-use development is built on the former Triple E Ranch. Beginning with the design phase, reducing the environmental impact of this development on the surrounding natural communities has been a priority. All the homes meet Energy Star standards, and the vast majority of the buildings and transportation infrastructure are situated on former cattle pastures. This allowed Harmony to preserve nearly all the wooded wetlands and forests. The developer also preserved the lakefront property as public land, protecting two five-hundred-acre lakes and their riparian ecosystems. Preserving these natural areas lowered development costs by reducing the amount of land-clearing required, and it simultaneously increased property values by creating a network of shared green spaces for the community. Because the pastureland was adjacent to the highway, focusing the development in this area has also increased exposure for this new community.

Another unusual way that Harmony's developer took advantage of previously disturbed land was by planning for a utility pipeline right-of-way to become a corridor connecting residents to distant natural areas and future neighborhoods. This low-intensity thoroughfare gives residents the freedom to walk, bike, or drive golf

(Continued on page 44)

Provide Wildlife with Food, Water, Cover, and Space

Functional wildlife habitat supplies food, water, cover, and space.

- *Food:* Best in its natural form; it should include a variety of food items.
- *Water:* Necessary for animals to drink, bathe in, and in some cases use for reproduction (e.g., frog eggs develop in water).
- *Cover:* Permits animals to escape from predators, and provides safety from natural disturbances such as storms. Animals also need cover in order to rest and for building nests and dens in order to raise young.
- *Space:* This is an area large enough to enable wildlife species to meet their daily requirements in terms of food, cover, and water, and to successfully raise their young. Connections across the land are important so that animals may move between habitats, creating healthy populations within a region.

Figure 7. Florida Natives sculpture along a sidewalk in the town of Harmony. Courtesy of Harmony Development Co.

carts around their community, thus avoiding the high-intensity access roads designed for cars. The developer also commissioned a piece of artwork, a sculpture called the *Florida Natives,* which symbolizes the agricultural history of the Triple E Ranch while promoting a connection with native plants and animals. The artist, Kia Ricchi, reused a former Triple E Ranch roller packer designed for pressing hayseed into the soil. The sculpture was placed along a sidewalk, and it depicts more than thirty different species of wildlife native to this region (Figure 7).

Source: H. Knowles and M.E. Hostetler, *Preserving Wildlife Habitat in Residential Developments* (Gainesville: Program for Resource Efficient Communities, University of Florida, 2005).

Different animal species prefer different types of habitat. Some species like forested areas, others prefer meadows or wetlands, and some prefer a combination of different habitats. Any design and management plan for a property must consider the target species. As mentioned, an inventory of the wildlife on a site will determine which species are present. This information will help to prioritize which habitats most need to be conserved. Any design and management plan will benefit some species and not others. When evaluating land for wildlife habitat, consider the following basic wildlife management and ecological concepts:

- Generalist versus specialist
- Big versus small
- Species' needs during different stages of life
- Metapopulations of wildlife

Generalist versus specialist. Animals that are generalists are species that eat a variety of items and live in a variety of habitats. Generalists typically adapt to new food sources and changed landscapes. House sparrows (*Passer domesticus*) and European starlings (*Sturnus vulgaris*), for example, eat a variety of foods and will readily use buildings for nesting. These birds are found throughout many countries outside their natural range in Europe, and are doing quite well in urban and agricultural areas. They seem to hold their own or even flourish when humans come into an area, as they are able to exploit new food sources, such as human food waste and seed feeders, and find new shelter areas like the eaves of buildings.

Specialists, on the other hand, have much more precise food and shelter requirements. Some eat only a few types of food and live in only one type of habitat. Many cannot tolerate human disturbances, such as traffic noise and light pollution. Overall, they do not adapt well to changes in their habitat and will go extinct locally (i.e., become extirpated) when their habitat changes. Endangered or threatened species tend to be specialists. Examples from the United States are most of the species listed on the U.S. lists of endangered and threatened species, such as the Florida panther (*Puma concolor coryi*). When evaluating a piece of property, conserving on-site habitat critical for a specialist is important, because specialists tend to be affected the most when humans move in.

Big versus small. The size of the animal is an important factor when trying to decide which areas to conserve. Larger animals operate at broader scales than smaller species and need more space to meet their daily requirements. This roaming area is called the animal's home range. A red-tailed hawk (*Buteo jamaicensis*) can roam over tens of miles looking for food and mates. In comparison, a small Carolina wren (*Thryothorus ludovicianus*) can spend an entire summer foraging in a few backyards (Box 4).

When preserving habitat for a large animal, whether a bird, mammal, or reptile, developers have to think about tens to hundreds of acres of land. A small patch of open space is not enough for a bear, but it may be fine for a small rodent. Furthermore, it is important to connect various natural areas both

---

Box 4. Habitat Selection: A Bird's-Eye View

If a red-tailed hawk appears in a residential neighborhood, it is there not only because of what is in that neighborhood but also because of what surrounds it. In general, red-tailed hawk habitat is a mixture of open and forested areas. At each scale (yard, neighborhood, town), the hawk responds to certain objects in a landscape, such as trees and open space. Within the yard, it may respond to large trees in which to nest or roost. In the neighborhood, it could be the amount of forested area and open space. Forested areas provide roosting spots, and open spaces provide areas to catch rodents and other prey animals. At the scale of the town, the hawk also responds to the forested and open areas, but it does this within a much larger area (Figure 8). One side of town may have a larger number of appropriate open areas and forested areas than another. The hawk may prefer one side of town and establish a home range in this area. In this example, the yard, neighborhood, and town form the range of scales at which the hawk responds to objects within a landscape. Each scale is an important factor in determining where the hawk locates itself, but of primary importance is what is going on at the scale of the town, because this limits where the hawk establishes its home range. Compare this to the needs of a Carolina wren, which operates on a much more limited range of scales. The structure within one backyard or several backyards influences where a wren establishes a home range (Figure 8).

Across a range of scales, different bird species respond to different objects within a landscape. The type of object a bird prefers depends on its natural history—what it eats, what it needs for nesting, and so on. One bird species might prefer tree patches, while another might prefer flowering plants. Some prefer woods along streams (riparian habitats), while others prefer natural open fields.

within and outside a site to permit animals with large home ranges to travel across the landscape. Wildlife corridors are important because they allow animals, especially mammals, amphibians, and reptiles, to traverse a landscape riddled with barriers such as roads, cities, and agricultural areas.

Species' needs during different stages of life. During different periods of an animal's life, it may have different requirements for food, water, cover, and space. For example, birds' requirements when breeding differ from their requirements when migrating or wintering in an area. Some bird species, such as

---

Even the actual buildings or landscaped yards in a neighborhood could provide suitable habitat for some bird species.

In general, the size of a bird limits the scales at which it responds to habitat structure. A connection exists between the decisions of people in a city and the distribution of birds. In the cases of the red-tailed hawk and the Carolina wren, policy makers and developers have the most influence on the distribution of hawks, whereas the decisions made by homeowners and developers significantly affect the distribution of wrens.

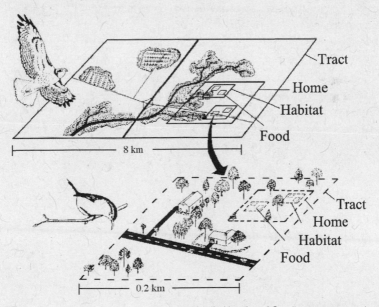

Figure 8. The range of scales at which a red-tailed hawk and Carolina wren respond to habitat features within an urban landscape. Drawing by Rebekah McClean.

the ovenbird (*Seiurus aurocapillus*), nest primarily in large expanses of wooded areas to keep their nests hidden from predators, catching insects to feed their young. However, outside the breeding season, this same bird species can be found in small patches of fragmented forest, feeding on a variety of food items including fruits and seeds.

After the breeding season, many young animals disperse from their natal sites looking for new areas that provide food and shelter. For such animals, urban sites may not be appropriate for breeding but could serve as dispersal sites, where animals feed and rest while searching for new habitat. These dispersal sites can serve as corridors or stepping stones that help animals move from one habitat to the next. In addition, urban sites can serve as stopover sites for birds seeking food and shelter along their migration route (Box 5). Natural urban patches also facilitate the movement of mammals, reptiles, amphibians, and insects. And urban area can serve as wintering sites for animals that traditionally breed outside of urban areas.

Box 5. Urban Stopover Sites for Migrating Birds

Natural patches in urban areas are used by a variety of birds, but some of these natural patches may not be appropriate nesting habitat for more sensitive species. They may, however, provide valuable foraging habitat for birds during migration. Studies indicate that many species of migrating birds use habitat in urban areas during the fall and spring migration. These urban stopover sites provide places for birds to rest, refuel, and shelter from predators. Neotropical migrating birds breed in the United States and Canada, and they overwinter in Central and South America. This is a long migration trip, and birds need to periodically stop along the migration route. Many cities are located along migration routes; in these areas, a large number of birds will drop out of the sky to rest and refuel. This is especially true of birds that fly across large water bodies and of those that fly along the coastline. Cities positioned on the shore of a large lake, such as Chicago, are prime spots for birds to stop and rest. Without sufficient vegetation cover for migrants stopping in urban cities, exhausted birds are vulnerable to predation and adverse climate conditions. Plus, without sufficient foraging opportunities, these birds may not be able to gain enough energy to continue migrating. Even single mature trees in backyards can provide opportunities for shelter and food. For example, cedar trees (*Juniperus virginiana*) have fruits that migrating birds eat. Although individual plants can play a role, larger natural patches attract a wider variety of avian species.

In summary, a particular property can serve as habitat for animals during different times of the year. An urban patch of woods may be a breeding area for some animals, while at other times it may serve as a stopover site or wintering site. In many cases, the property may serve primarily as an important connector between natural areas, permitting the movement of animals.

Metapopulations and wildlife. The health of wildlife populations is a result of the complex interaction of separate populations within a given region. In its most simplified version, a metapopulation is a group of animals that are separated from one another by some distance. Occasionally individuals from one group migrate to another group. These metapopulations are essential to maintaining healthy regional populations. One reason these separate but somewhat connected populations are important is the resilience to catastrophic disturbances. Natural disturbances such as fire, flood, disease, and hurricanes can wipe out individuals in an area. After a disturbance, individuals from the

---

How big a patch is needed to attract a wide variety of species? That is an open question, but it is safe to say the bigger the better. For many terrestrial bird species, conservation actions should include conserving and restoring tree canopy cover, as well as efforts to conserve natural habitat below the tree canopy—that is, to increase vertical height diversity. Riparian habitats—areas along the shores of lakes and rivers—are particularly attractive to migrating birds, and natural vegetation along water bodies should be a target for conservation. Conserved natural areas must be managed in a way that minimizes the human impact on these areas. This includes controlling feral cats and dogs, reducing the amount of walking trails through these areas, preventing invasive exotic plants from spreading, and eliminating off-road vehicles in these areas. To serve as a significant stopover patch for migrating birds, a natural area must be managed to limit the amount of disturbance that occurs near its center.

Sources: J.D. Brawn and D.F. Stotz, "The importance of the Chicago region and the 'Chicago Wilderness' initiative for avian conservation," in *Avian Ecology and Conservation in an Urbanizing World*, ed. J.M. Marzluff, R. Bowman, and R. Donnelly, pp. 509–522 (Boston: Kluwer Academic Publications, 2000); M.E. Hostetler, S. Duncan, and J. Paul, "The effects of an apartment complex on migrating and wintering birds," *Southeastern Naturalist* 4 (2005): 421–434; M. E. Hostetler and C.S. Holling, "Detecting the scales at which birds respond to structure in urban landscapes," *Urban Ecosystems* 4 (2000): 25–54.

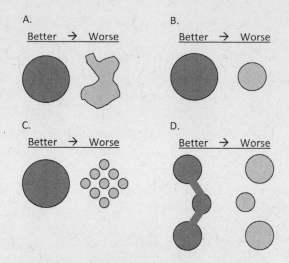

FIGURE 9. Optimal patch designs conserve habitat for species that are specialists. Circular patches (*a*) are better than other shapes. Large patches (*b*) are better than small. One large patch (*c*) is better than several small patches with the same total area. Patches connected by corridors (*d*) are better than those without. Illustration by Hal Knowles III.

other populations can colonize this area and reestablish a healthy population of animals. If the entire population of a species were located in one area, an epidemic or other natural disaster could wipe out the population. The existence of separate populations guards against this scenario. A piece of property may serve as an important habitat for a metapopulation, especially if it is connected to other habitats in the region.

Patch size, shape, and connectivity are important factors when determining which habitats to preserve for species, so it is imperative to designate conservation areas according to ecological principles. As mentioned, wildlife species that are declining tend to be specialists, they need a specific type of habitat, and they are more vulnerable to daily human disturbances. Specialists typically do not do well in fragmented areas consisting of relatively small, remnant patches. In fragmented areas, small natural remnants are not buffered enough against human disturbances and are more exposed to traffic, noise, and artificial lights. Following are four general principles that address preserving habitat for species that are specialists (see also Figure 9).

A. *Circular patches are better than other shapes.* This helps to minimize edge effects. Wildlife living in habitat edges tend to encounter higher levels of predation, higher levels of human disturbance, and increased competition from other species. Specialists often avoid patches with lots of edge. However, some wildlife species (mainly generalists) prefer edge habitat and thrive in these areas.[8]

The transition between built and conserved natural areas should be "soft." In general, "soft" transitions act as a buffer between the "hard" urban areas and a natural community or wildlife corridor. One example might be a landscaped community park or naturalistic stormwater pond separating a large parking lot from a protected natural area. In transitional areas, the disparities between urban and natural areas—such as the difference between the bright lights of urban areas and the low light of natural areas at night—can be minimized. The transitional areas help filter the light and prevent it from reaching conserved natural areas.

B. *Large patches are better than small.* As a general rule, bigger patches tend to have more species. Many specialist species, such as some forest songbirds, primarily live in interior habitat during the breeding season.[9] How far the edge effects extend into a patch is variable and depends on the species in question, the type of disturbance, and the types of vegetation found along an edge. For example, varied thrushes (*Ixoreusn aeviu*) had lower relative densities up to 140 meters into a patch.[10]

C. *One large patch is better than several small patches with the same total area.* Simply totaling the area of conserved wildlife habitat on a development property is insufficient. Small, fragmented patches have more edge habitat and may not provide adequate space to sustain many specialist species. Some animals require large expanses of unfragmented habitat to survive, whereas others can survive quite well in fragmented areas. Generally, though, many declining species are negatively affected by fragmentation, and a good strategy is to conserve as large a patch as possible.

D. *Patches connected by corridors are better than those without.* Evidence shows that landscape connectivity plays an important role in the survival and stability of individual species and even entire ecosystems (Box 6). For wildlife, corridors can serve two purposes. First, connections allow animals to reach diverse habitats within their home ranges; and second, at a broader scale, connections permit occasional movements between somewhat isolated populations of wildlife. It is best to make an effort to preserve habitat that has functional connections to other existing natural communities. Whenever possible, habitat preservation should be coordinated with adjacent landowners. This can help to create a matrix of natural areas suitable for both localized and wide-ranging species. When incorporating wildlife corridors into a master plan, use the following general rules:

Box 6. Corridors, Birds, and Plant Diversity

A unique landscape-scale study on the effects of corridors on plant and animal dispersal has shown that patches connected by corridors promoted both the dispersal of plant seeds and bird movement. The researchers cut out four patches within a dense pine plantation matrix; one patch was connected to a central patch measuring one hundred meters by one hundred meters, while three other patches were not connected to this central patch. This central patch was planted with wax myrtle bushes (*Myrica cerifera*), which produce berries frequently eaten by eastern bluebirds (*Sialia sialis*). Bluebirds generally prefer open habitat, and this was shown when researchers tracked bluebirds in this study. These birds tend to fly parallel to edges of cleared patches. Placing seed traps on poles in each of the patches where birds perched and defecated into them—researchers found that the connected patch had 37 percent more seed from the central patch than the unconnected patches had. The corridor edge helped funnel the bluebirds from the central patch to the connected patch.

Tracking plant species diversity over five years, researchers found that the connected patches initially had plant diversity similar to that of the other patches. By the end of the study though, the connected patch had 20 percent more plant species than unconnected patches. The understory of the connected patches was much more species-rich than that of the unconnected patches as a result of increased seed deposition by birds and pollen movement. These results suggest that corridors can promote biodiversity within fragmented landscapes.

Sources: D.J. Levey, B.M. Bolker, J.J. Tewksbury, S. Sargent, and N.M. Haddad, "Effects of landscape corridors on seed dispersal by birds," *Science* 309 (2005): 146–148; E.I. Damschen, N.M. Haddad, J.L. Orrock, J.J. Tewksbury, and D.J. Levey. "Corridors increase plant species richness at large scales," *Science* 313 (2006): 1284–1286.

- Natural landscape connections that are already established and used as movement corridors for wildlife are better than new, human-made connections. Rivers, streams, shelter belts, hedges, field boundaries, and road and rail edges may all act as preferential pathways for wildlife and plant dispersal. These linear features may be continuous, as in the case of rivers, or fragmented, as in the case of hedges, which could be used as stepping-stones. Many terrestrial species are capable of walking or flying between closely aligned patches. Predator control may be needed along these connective corridors, as they may be used by nonnative predators, such as cats, as well as by native predators.

- Wide corridors are better than narrow corridors. Interior conditions are more likely to be present throughout the centers of wide corridors. In contrast, narrow corridors are typically all edge habitat, and so do not buffer as well against human disturbances. When relatively wide corridors are not possible, even narrow corridors are beneficial to some species.

- Typically, areas along streams and rivers provide the most productive corridors, because a variety of species use them. In some regions, almost 70 percent of all vertebrate species use riparian areas at some point during their life cycles. Useful riparian corridors include areas of upland forest on at least one bank, in addition to the entire floodplain on both banks. During flood events, animals can still use the upland areas. When providing walking, cycling, or horse-riding paths along linear features such as river floodplains, ensure that the paths don't take up only the best, most central and productive part of the corridor; protect portions of all aspects of the environment and the experience. Human trails should be situated mainly on the edges of corridors to reduce disturbance, fragmentation, and other edge effects. Careful consideration must be given to the mixed use of a corridor, because human traffic can affect wildlife species and their use of the corridor.

Although these recommendations are the best-case scenarios, it is important to recognize that not all developments can be designed to follow these recommendations. A site may permit conservation of only relatively small, scattered natural patches with narrow corridors. While such patches may have limited appeal for some of the larger animals and the specialists, they may still serve as habitat for smaller species such as lizards, frogs, and insects. Any connections are better than no connections, as they may permit wildlife and even plants to spread from one remnant to the next. Small remnants and corridors will also contain a variety of plants and soil biota, such as millipedes. *Any opportunity to conserve even the smallest patch should be considered, because small natural areas contain a diversity of organisms that will be retained on-site.* Removing even the smallest natural areas that could have been conserved will, in effect, decrease biodiversity in the area. After-the-fact restoration efforts, such as planting with natives, will not instantly restore the original biota found there, but these little areas could serve as sources of seeds and critters that could spread to other areas of the site after construction. Over time, the biodiversity of a site with conserved patches will be much better compared to a site that was scraped clean and planted with an assortment of natives.

Based on the aforementioned ecological principles, a good subdivision design would plan for conserving biodiversity in large, connected patches of habitat and would locate building sites in one concentrated area. This is a challenge, because designing a compact development that sets aside large, natural areas can run contrary to local wetland regulations. Often local policies will require the protection of any wetland or ephemeral depression, and the developer will have to build around them. This can result in a shredded site plan, with wetlands interspersed among built areas (Box 7). A fragmented landscape is not conducive to conserving some of the more sensitive plant and animal species. Such a plan would increase the amount of impervious surfaces, because a more linear design would require additional roads for automobiles. Small, fragmented wetlands and conserved upland areas would be surrounded by built landscapes and prone to daily impact by nearby homes and streets, such as stormwater runoff). Designating larger conserved areas, separated as much as possible from built areas, makes management of the conserved areas easier, and such a design helps buffer against built-area impacts. Choosing a compact design often means that some wetlands will have to be filled in, and current policies usually levy stiff fines when wetlands are destroyed. A compromise would be to use dilapidated wetland areas for stormwater mitigation, such as by building retention ponds. Using native plants and pond designs that maximize wildlife habitat (e.g., littoral zones for wading birds) can increase the biodiversity value of degraded wetland areas.

It is imperative to conserve any natural communities that are threatened. Priority must be given to rare natural communities. For example, there may be few prairie remnants left in a region, and if prairie grassland exists on a site, priority should be given to this vegetative community. It may be that several natural community types that are rare in a region exist on a site. As in most complex issues, there are no steadfast rules: nothing mandates that a certain natural community must always be preserved ahead of another. Each decision must take into consideration the particular parcel of land. Quantity is not necessarily better than quality; in some situations, a high-quality though

---

Box 7. Compact versus Fragmented Subdivision

Restoration is the name of a 5,181-acre *conservation* community proposed within the city of Edgewater, Florida, just west of I-95 and north of Daytona. It is a master-planned new town that will consist of eighty-five hundred residential units and buildings for commercial, office, and light industrial uses. In 2005, the developer entered into discussions with the city of Edgewater, the St. Johns River Water Management District, and the East Central Florida Regional Planning Council about developing the property. On the west side of the property lies a fragile wetland system called Spruce Creek Swamp. If the developer were to avoid building on wetlands, and built only on uplands, this hypothetical plan would place 75' x 130' lots across the entire site. This plan was named the "Swiss Cheese Plan" because development is scattered throughout the site (Figure 10a).

In this hypothetical development plan, residential homes and a major road were situated in upland areas very near to Spruce Creek Swamp and other environmental systems. With homes and roads fragmenting the landscape, this design could neither protect wildlife nor promote water quality through the conservation of natural sheet flows across the property. During the negotiations and discussions with the aforementioned agencies and several scientists from the University of Florida, the developer went through several design iterations, making the proposed built areas more compact and moving them from the western area of the property to the eastern, closer to I-95 (Figure 10b). Much of the site is degraded forestland, and as part of the plan for the site the wetlands and upland habitats have been marked for restoration. Longleaf pines will be replanted and drainage ditches and canals will be eliminated. More than 3,400 acres are now protected in conserved areas, and a large buffer has been designated to help protect Spruce Creek Swamp on the west side of the property. The final plan contains eighty-five hundred residential units, the same number proposed in the "Swiss Cheese Plan." Built areas will feature low-impact development techniques, such as a distributed stormwater treatment system containing swales and enhanced retention ponds. This example

(Continued on page 56)

demonstrates that collaborations among academics, developers, and policy makers can result in a compact conservation community with the potential to not only conserve biodiversity but also restore it

(a)

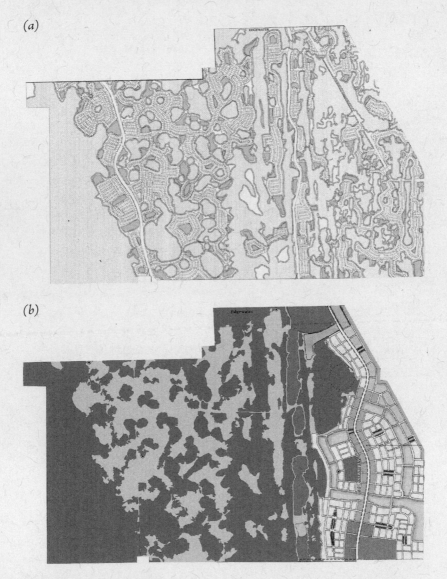

(b)

Figure 10.   In a hypothetical Swiss cheese design (*a*), built lots occupy all the upland areas, avoiding wetlands, which results in a highly fragmented development. In a hypothetical compact design layout (*b*), all built areas are clustered near a highway on the east side, and the west side is conserved land. (Light gray indicates uplands; dark gray indicates wetlands.) Courtesy of Canin Associates.

somewhat common natural community may be preferable for preservation over a low-quality rare community.

When a piece of property is environmentally significant, a conservation easement could be placed on it to preserve its natural areas. Conservation easements are among the smartest ways to conserve important natural, historic, or agricultural resources and protect natural heritage. A conservation easement limits the amount of development on a designated parcel of land and is a legal agreement between a landowner and a land trust, government agency, or other entity. This agreement stipulates that the land will remain in its present state; future development is prohibited.

Conservation easements offer great flexibility. Each conservation easement is typically customized in consultations between the landowner and the partner organization. It takes into consideration both the landowner's needs and the conservation objectives. Such easements may be designed to allow continued farming or ranching activities, hunting, and other recreational uses (Box 8). An easement can apply to just a portion of a property. In most cases, conservation easements are perpetual, so any land use restrictions remain if the land is sold or passed on to heirs. Typically, future development rights are restricted and are recorded on the deed. Essentially, a conservation easement protects the preferences of the current landowner and formally stipulates what can happen to the property in the future.

Conservation easements are managed by federal, state, and local governmental agencies, as well as by nongovernmental organizations. Although all such easements are similar in principle, different organizations may have different priorities, depending on their missions, and these priorities will influence the type and degree of land use restrictions required in the easement. Some organizations may prioritize the protection of large natural areas, while the goal of others may be to maintain agricultural lands in production. Land Trust Alliance (www.lta.org) maintains a Web page that lists a variety of land trust organizations in each state.

For the landowner, various types of financial benefits are available with conservation easements. Easements may result in direct payments, tax relief, and reduction of estate taxes when passing land to heirs. In the United States, four potential tax savings are associated with donating a conservation easement: income tax, real property tax, federal gift and estate tax, and estate tax exclusion. The rules for these tax savings do change from year to year. In 2010, Congress renewed the enhanced tax incentive for conservation easement, and

Box 8. Keeping the Working Land Working

Near Boston, Georgia, Joseph Moody Jr., a landowner, donated 537 acres to Tall Timbers Land Conservancy, located in Florida (www.talltimbers.org/landconservancy.html). Portions of the farm have been in the Moody family since 1876, and several significant longleaf pine (*Pinus palustris*) ecosystems are located on the property. Mr. Moody's farm continues to be a working farm, with cotton, peanuts, and pecans. In order to better conserve the natural areas on the property, various land management practices have been implemented. Prescribed burns are executed to maintain the longleaf pine ecosystem (Figure 11). The cultivation practice of tilling cropland, which turns over the soil, has been eliminated to help control agriculture runoff into nearby wetlands. As Mr. Moody stated, "I wanted to maintain the property in its present form as long as possible. Conservation easement—this is forever."

Figure 11. Longleaf pine ecosystem maintained by prescribed burns on the property of Joseph Moody Jr., near Boston, Georgia. Photo by the author.

it increased the tax benefits of donating a voluntary conservation agreement. These incentives make it easier for average Americans—including working family farmers and ranchers—to donate land. The legislation

- raises the maximum deduction a donor may take, from 30 percent of his or her income in any year to 50 percent;
- enables qualifying farmers and ranchers to deduct up to 100 percent of their adjusted gross income; and
- allows donors to take deductions for their contribution for a maximum of sixteen years.

These incentives allow many modest-income landowners to deduct much more than they could under the old rules, increasing the fairness of the tax code. The law also tightens appraisal standards, which were sometimes abused by landowners collaborating with appraisers to unfairly increase their deductions. The Land Trust Alliance usually has updated information about easements on its Web site.

Construction Phase

Minimize Soil Disturbance

It sometimes takes thousands of years to form healthy soils and habitats; destroying them can take only hours. Even removing functioning topsoil, storing it on-site, and returning it to the original location does not conserve it. Removing soil is such a disruptive process that it destroys soil structure; it takes years for the soil to return to its original state. On disturbed sites that need soil enhancements, care should be taken to use only soil from other locations within the construction site or from nearby sources. The following tips describe ways to minimize soil disturbance during the construction phase.[11]

1. Use construction site access and routes that coincide with the eventual streets and roads. This will limit compaction of the soil to areas that will contain roadways for the subdivision. Vehicle routes should be clearly marked.
2. Designate parking and stockpiling sites for vehicles and building materials. Areas must be clearly marked so contractors know where to park vehicles and to store materials.

3. Minimize staging areas for the construction of buildings. Equipment and building materials should be stored in areas that are planned for future hardscapes, such as patios, pavement, and so on.

4. Mix chemicals and materials only in designated areas that are properly managed, because even small chemical spills can leach into the ground and affect soil chemistry and inhibit plant growth.

5. Install significant fencing to protect significant areas. Yellow plastic tape is not enough.

6. Avoid lowering or raising the grade around trees and in natural areas, as lowering the grade damages roots, and raising the grade smothers them (see the "Save Individual Trees" section later in this chapter).

7. Do not bury utilities in protected areas. Utilities should be placed in shared trenches dug near or under pavement.

Box 9. Aurora Development Construction Covenants, Whittlesea, Australia

This is a unique partnership between a large developer, VicUrban; EPA Victoria; Yarra Valley Water; and the City of Whittlesea. VicUrban is the Victorian government's new sustainable urban development agency, and its first major development project is the Aurora community, located just outside of Melbourne, Australia. Approximately eighty-five hundred units are planned, which will house more than twenty-five thousand people. The development has many sustainability goals to address biodiversity,

Figure 12. This emblem depicts natural resource and conservation issues for the Aurora development project, Whittlesea, Australia. Courtesy of VicUrban.

water, energy, and waste issues (Figure 12; for details, see www.vicurban.com). VicUrban has undertaken an inventory of the site and has identified habitats and species that are to be conserved.

8. Carefully select equipment used on a site. The use of heavy equipment compacts and disrupts the soil more than necessary. Alternative equipment and systems, such as pole slings and tripods with block and tackle, could be used to move heavy slabs or pieces of rock.[12] In many cases, the equipment, such as motorized augers for postholes, can be carried by hand.

9. Develop covenants and contracts for site construction, and have all contractors and subcontractors who come onto the site sign these agreements (Box 9). In particular, contracts should clearly identify areas and landscape features that are protected, and include financial penalties for contractors who damage these areas. During construction, punitive measures should be in place to penalize contractors who drive vehicles outside delineated routes for heavy vehicles. Bonuses could be stipulated for contractors who do no damage to protected areas.

In addition to undertaking environmental planning and monitoring efforts, the developer has created covenants with the three governmental entities to address sustainable construction-site methods. These are the most thorough environmental covenants that I have found signed by a development entity and local government agencies. Following are some of the covenants:

- Install infrastructure for using recycled water for toilet flushing and irrigation.
- Incorporate water-sensitive urban design principles to improve stormwater quality.
- Provide training and education for the builders and their subcontractors in ways to avoid and manage waste in Aurora.
- Protect large trees and other valued vegetation throughout the construction phase, and plant new trees to achieve a net gain.
- Develop and provide additional information illustrating how householder practices can also contribute to the ongoing sustainability of a development.
- Maintain and enhance indigenous flora and fauna species and communities, along with the habitats that support these species and communities.
- Research and document local environmental conditions (e.g., local climate and soil characteristics) and promote awareness among all stakeholders, including new residents.

Source: *Aurora Sustainability Covenant*, 2006, www.epa.vic.gov.au/bus/sustainability_covenants/aurora.asp.

Reduce, Reuse, and Recycle Materials On-Site

The concept of preserving natural areas extends beyond the boundary of a property. It is easy to see the benefits of preserving natural habitat on a development site, yet the efficient use of building resources can also preserve habitat in distant locations, where the resource-harvesting takes place. At points around the world, wildlife habitat is being degraded to create building products and urban landscapes. By limiting the amount of virgin resources that are extracted to build a development, energy, water, and land can be conserved elsewhere.

Save Individual Trees

Individual trees, particularly native species, are important to conserve.[13] Many plants and animals use a single tree as habitat, and it takes a long time to grow a mature tree. To help preserve large or significant trees, a developer and hired contractors can do several things during the construction process. First, protect as much of the root zone as possible from heavy vehicles; one method to do this is to install a fence under the outer branches of a tree (i.e., around the drip line). This will protect about half of the tree's roots from damage (Figure 13).

Even with this drip line method, 50 percent or more of the roots will still be affected by construction. The best way to help insure the survival of a protected tree is to irrigate it. Stressed trees need plenty of water during the construction process, and this often requires watering the entire area inside the drip line of each tree to a soil depth of twelve inches, about two or three times per week. Organic mulch spread four to six inches in depth within the tree protection zone helps maintain soil moisture. Mulch should not be placed up against the tree trunk, because doing so will promote fungus growth on the trunk. Next, if roots must be pruned at the edge of the root-protection zone, a tool called an air spade can be used to open up a trench with minimal damage to the roots. Roots should then be cleanly cut with a saw. Lowering or raising the soil grade around trees (particularly in the root protection zone) even a few inches can effectively kill the tree. Lowering the grade a few inches will remove important root mass and raising the grade a few inches will smother roots by preventing oxygen from reaching them. Finally, under no circumstances should heavy machinery be allowed to run over the soil within the tree protection zone. Over 90 percent of the relative compaction of the soil occurs within the first three passes over a patch of soil.[14] Hiring a certified arborist

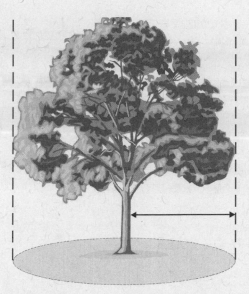

FIGURE 13. The shaded circle represents where a fence should be located to protect about 50 percent of a tree's root mass. This method is appropriate for trees with broad crowns. Courtesy of the Program for Resource Efficient Communities.

to oversee tree management can go a long way toward protecting the health of preserved trees.

Protect Riparian Areas along Streams and Rivers

Riparian areas stabilize stream banks, limit erosion, reduce flood-size flows, and filter and settle out runoff pollutants. Riparian areas are also important habitat for a variety of wildlife species. For any given waterway, the width of the riparian area required (called a setback or buffer) will vary depending on local site conditions and goals—for example, is the buffer to prevent soil erosion or provide wildlife habitat? For filtration of surface flow (the runoff entering the stream), some experts recommend that a minimum of 30 meters of vegetative buffer is needed;[15] this will achieve 70 percent of pollutant removal or more, depending on vegetation, soil composition, and slope.[16] For wildlife habitat, depending on the location and species, the buffer should extend between 140 meters and 300 meters from the stream edge, and sometimes farther than this.[17]

Use Construction Techniques to Minimize Human-Wildlife Conflicts

A developer must recognize that, whatever the design of a residential subdivision, it may result in future wildlife-human conflicts. Subdividing the land automatically increases the amount of edge habitat, which can result in overabundant populations of certain problematic wildlife species.[18] A compact design with built areas located in one area, and a large natural patch in another area, is one way to limit edges. However, even in a subdivision design that limits edges, several species of animals will find the houses and artificial sources of food irresistible. Raccoons, bats, and squirrels find ways to enter and reside in attics and crawl spaces. Garbage cans become a food source for bears, raccoons, and even squirrels. Animals using artificial den sites and food sources can come into direct conflict with people and their pets. Stormwater ponds attract ducks and geese, and if people feed these birds, the ducks and geese can become overabundant and their droppings will foul waterways, lawns, and sidewalks. Deer are known to eat a variety of ornamental plants, resulting in extra time and money spent to replace damaged plants. Thus, a few wildlife species can become a nuisance, and residents may have to spend a lot of time and money to resolve conflicts.

Homes, waste disposal systems, and even stormwater treatment systems could be built to minimize human-wildlife conflicts. While no perfect solution exists, developers can be cognizant of the potential of wildlife-human conflicts. Opportunities exist during the construction phase to minimize future conflicts. Case in point: raccoons commonly inhabit chimneys.[19] To exclude raccoons from chimneys, builders can add chimney caps at the time of home construction. The attic ventilation systems in homes can be made much sturdier to prevent bat and squirrel intrusions. Where warranted, household and neighborhood refuse containers can be made raccoon and bear proof, and developers should build or purchase such containers. Bear-proof waste containers can help prevent bears from entering urban areas to obtain food. Studies have indicated that bears enter urban areas not primarily because of a population increase, but because garbage lures them into a neighborhood.[20]

The design of stormwater retention ponds can help prevent the overabundance of ducks and geese. Turfgrass installed right up to the edges of ponds is attractive to ducks and geese. Grass is a food source for some ducks and geese, and they find that the ability to exit directly from the water to feed is alluring. In general, Canada geese (*Branta canadensis*) will not nest in ponds when they cannot easily walk in and out of the water. Planting dense bushes and small trees along the edge can form an effective barrier. Installing trees around ponds will disrupt the flight path of waterfowl and make ponds less attractive for resting and feeding. In more open landscapes, groups of trees and shrubs that limit a bird's view to less than ten meters will make an area less attractive to geese and ducks.[21]

When choosing plants for landscaping, developers should keep in mind that deer are notorious for munching on a variety of ornamental plants. Tulips are like "deer candy," but deer will also eat less palatable plants when natural browse is scarce because of a population explosion or other reasons. In regions with lots of deer, one should select plants that are deer resistant to prevent future homeowner frustrations with these animals. Each region of the country has a variety of ornamental plants available for use in urban landscapes, and some of these plants are deer resistant. Lists of deer-resistant plant species can be found at the following Web sites:

- Oregon State University, "Deer-Resistant Ornamental Plants," http://extension.oregonstate.edu/catalog/pdf/ec/ec1440.pdf
- University of Florida, "Ornamental Plant Susceptibility to Damage by Deer in Florida," http://edis.ifas.ufl.edu/uw137
- North Carolina University, "Deer Resistant Plants," http://pender.ces.ncsu.edu/files/library/71/Deer%20Resistant%20Plants.pdf
- Washington State University, "Deer Resistant Plants," www.spokane-county.wsu.edu

One noteworthy concern is the danger of contractors feeding wildlife during the construction process. Feeding wildlife ultimately causes animals to lose their fear of humans, and when they do, it can be dangerous to both animals and people. As an example, in Florida, it is almost guaranteed that an alligator will eventually move into a stormwater retention pond created during construction. If the alligators are present during build-out, contractors should be warned that feeding these animals could cause a dangerous situation. Once an alligator is fed, it loses its fear of humans and is more apt to approach people looking for handouts. If it is a large animal, such close encounters can put people in danger, especially small children, as well as pets. Such a scenario happened in the town of Harmony, Florida. Homeowners noticed that a few alligators were coming out of the ponds and approaching residents. The tameness of these alligators was most likely a result of contractors feeding them during construction (Greg Golgowski, Harmony's conservation manager, personal communication, 2007). Unfortunately, the large alligators had to be euthanized because of the risk they posed to humans. Even small mammals, such as raccoons and squirrels, when fed by contractors or by open waste containers can ultimately become a nuisance for homeowners who move into a neighborhood. Thus, developers should educate contractors about the ramifications of feeding wildlife, and strict guidelines about food disposal should be followed to limit the availability of artificial food sources throughout a construction site.

Limit Construction Activity during Times of Significant Wildlife Activity

On a construction site, there may be wildlife habitats where significant wildlife species would be affected by construction activity. During times of the year when these areas are used by wildlife species, a temporary hold on construction in their vicinity should be scheduled. The life cycle of many organisms may be disrupted by construction activities, warranting a cessation of building homes or other infrastructure. For example, some secretive marsh birds, such as bitterns, have nesting sites in marsh areas of rivers, ponds, and lakes. Breeding typically occurs in the spring and summer, and depending on local conditions and the species, the noise of construction vehicles and people may disrupt the breeding activity of these birds.[22] As a result, some species may cease nesting in the area. Furthermore, certain habitats may be significant stopover sites for migrating birds, and nearby construction activities may disrupt their foraging and resting opportunities. In such situations, construction in the vicinity should cease during spring and fall migration. Even the life cycles of aquatic organisms, such as spawning, may be affected by construction, such as when silt runs off the land and into the spawning area. Each development site will be different, but by identifying areas of significant wildlife activity, one can locate construction activity away from sensitive areas.

Use Contractors and Subcontractors Trained in Sustainable Practices

It is crucial to have trained and motivated contractors and subcontractors who will properly implement a plan—I cannot stress this enough.[23] Often, these groups of professionals are not brought in during planning and are not fully engaged or do not understand the conservation priorities of the project. Without trained or fully engaged contractors or landscapers, many things can happen during the construction phase that could affect the viability of on-site or nearby natural habitat. And when plans have to be modified, construction site managers must be fully engaged and aware of practices that influence biodiversity. A construction manager who has read and understood the principles and suggestions in this book can more readily anticipate construction practices or accidents that might compromise the ability of the development to promote biodiversity. Construction supervisors and all tradespeople and built environment professionals should take an educational course that addresses biodiversity and environmental issues that may arise during construction. Both private and public institutions administer such courses (see an example of continuing education courses taught at the University of Florida, www.buildgreen .ufl.edu).

It takes constant vigilance to properly manage construction activities on the site. All that is necessary to compromise the plan is one errant heavy vehicle running over a fence that is protecting a tree or natural area. In particular, silt fences should be carefully maintained to prevent water from running off the site. It has been conservatively estimated that, on construction sites, the rate of topsoil erosion occurs more than two thousand times faster than on normal vegetated soils.[24] Runoff can carry vast amounts of silt into a wetland and essentially choke the wetland to death. Silt fences must be routinely checked and repaired when they have fallen down or been damaged.

Postconstruction

Establish a Long-Term Educational and Management Program

If trails are located in conserved natural areas, a signage system should be established to inform people about the importance of staying on the trails and about human behaviors that could affect animals and plants. If feral cat colonies were to become established in the conserved areas, or even in the built areas nearby, they would have a significant negative impact on wildlife. Cats and dogs are known to harass and kill wildlife. In order to maintain healthy natural areas, residents will have to understand and be engaged in the proper management of yards, neighborhoods, and open space. For instance, many upland habitats require prescribed burns every few years, which means that nearby homeowners must understand and accept the necessity of prescribed fires (Box 10). Fire is a natural process in many ecosystems, such as Southern California chaparral and coastal sage scrub, and homeowners within such systems must become aware of proper home defense and the risk of fire. Further, if invasive exotic plants were initially removed, reinvasion will probably occur. Areas outside the development probably house invasive plants, so the potential for reinvasion is high. Residents need to know how to recognize and remove invasive exotic plants, because management over the long term is what determines whether invasive plants and animals will be controlled.

Any conserved areas will definitely need to be managed for many years, and this will take money. Several options exist to fund management activities. First, a portion of the lot sales could help establish a source of funding; factoring in interest, this could provide long-term cash for management activities such as prescribed burns. Another method is to require that a portion of homeowners association fees be allocated to management of the natural areas and maintenance of the educational signs. These funding mechanisms could be prescribed by the developer and codified in deed restrictions.

WHAT CAN A POLICY MAKER DO?

To protect significant natural areas within residential and commercial areas, a county or city must have a plan that identifies significant natural areas and directs growth to appropriate areas. When setting aside portions of

---

Box 10. Prescribed Fire and Neighborhoods

Fire is an important process in many ecosystems; flatwoods and dry prairies are adapted to fire, and many plant species, such as the wildflower prairie coreopsis (*Coreopsis palmata*), require periodic fires to maintain prominence within an area. Several wildlife species, too, such as the eastern meadowlark (*Sturnella magna*), are adapted to open landscapes and require periodic regeneration by fire. However, once residential neighborhoods become embedded in natural areas that require burning, it is often difficult to conduct prescribed burns. Many people do not like the idea of prescribed burns near neighborhoods, even though prescribed fires reduce the risk of larger, damaging fires in the future. Without a reduction of the fuel load in the surrounding habitat, a fire, when it does happen, is likely to be much more dangerous, because such fires burn very hot and can leap into nearby neighborhoods.

If a natural area must be burned periodically, nearby homeowners must be engaged and must understand the benefits of prescribed burns. Prescribed burns can reduce the risk of catastrophic fires, and at the same time, they benefit the natural ecosystem by opening up the understory and helping to regenerate endemic plants in the area. In Illinois, workshops led by a conservation manager in a development called Prairie Crossing helped to inform and engage residents in order to conduct prescribed burns near home lots (Figure 14).

developable land to improve connectivity between natural areas across a city or county, policy makers can help developers select these areas for conservation. Typically developers do not look beyond the boundaries of their development, and it is up to policy makers to guide landowners who want to subdivide their property. The way properties fit into the broader landscape can be important in terms of retaining local ecological function. For instance, developable land may be situated between two significant natural areas, and only by looking at the bigger picture will it be possible to identify where a corridor should be located to link the two areas and, by doing so, promote wildlife movement and the persistence of indigenous flora. Moreover, cities and counties should look outside their boundaries and view their own landscapes within the context of their region or state.

There are a number of programs and policies that local governments can use to promote the conservation of natural areas. These growth management

Figure 14.   A prescribed fire burns in a Prairie Crossing neighborhood, Illinois. Photo by Mike Sands.

Source: T.K. McGee, "Urban residents' approval of management measures to mitigate wildland-urban interface fire risks in Edmonton, Canada," *Landscape and Urban Planning* 82(4) (2007): 247–256.

measures occur at two scales: (1) conserving natural areas in land already slated for development, and (2) conserving natural areas across a city or county, essentially directing where residential subdivisions can be built and designating areas that are off-limits to development. Typically, management involves some form of growth control. The Environmental Law Institute published a really good book that summarizes the various policies and case studies that emphasize biodiversity conservation.[25] For the purposes of this discussion, I will concentrate primarily on polices that affect land already designated for development. Some of the more common growth management strategies include the following:

1. *Alternative zoning ordinances:* A variety of alternative zoning ordinances can improve biodiversity conservation on land zoned for development.
    a. *Overlay zones:* Zoning standards can be supplemented with an overlay zone. Essentially, where significant natural areas are identified, developers of properties in overlay zones may also be required to preserve specific natural features, such as patches of natural areas or particular wildlife populations.
    b. *Cluster development:* An applicable zoning ordinance may allow or require cluster development. This type of development preserves existing natural areas on a property by limiting development to a specific portion of the property. Sometimes allowable development densities may be increased to encourage clustering. Several cities have developed policies that provide financial incentives to developers who cluster homes and conserve open space (Box 11).
2. *Impact fees:* These fees are a mechanism for making owners of new developments responsible for a share of the new public service infrastructure required for newly added homes in the area. This reduces the financial impact on current residents by transferring a portion of the costs to the homeowners of the new development. A portion of impact fees can be designated for open space conservation.
3. *Community development districts:* CDDs are part of a special-purpose unit of local government that can be used to assist the delivery of urban community development services, such as landscaping, parks, infrastructure, and the preservation and management of natural areas (Box 12). With a CDD, natural open space can be conserved by selling it to the county. More information and an example of CDDs can be found at the Florida

Box 11. Open Space Subdivisions Policy

The following policy was implemented March 20, 2001, in Brevard County, Florida (2005 population 531,250, per the U.S. Census Bureau).

Purpose
To preserve open space by offering incentives to developers.

Summary
The ordinance is voluntary and provides incentives for creating open space in subdivisions. Developers may increase the density of residential lots by up to 25 percent if they cluster built lots and leave a certain percentage of open space. The ordinance applies to single-family zoning classifications.

Key provisions in the ordinance include the following: (1) the ordinance allows single-family residential development with reduced lot sizes and widths and a density bonus of up to 25 percent above the maximum building-lot yield, (2) it requires preservation of a minimum of 35 to 50 percent—depending on site conditions—of primary open space (preserved wetland and floodplain) and secondary open space (uplands), depending on the zoning of the property, (3) minimum residential lot sizes can range from four thousand square feet to one acre, (4) the ordinance requires developers to create and preserve interconnected open space by clustering homes, building narrower streets, making smaller lot sizes, and reducing impervious surfaces, (5) it requires the use of a four-step site design technique—identify land to be protected, locate individual house sites, connect sites with streets and trails, and draw lot lines—to preserve open space, (6) it requires subdivision designs to include pedestrian and bicycle trail systems, preserved wetlands, permanent conservation easements, and long-term open-space-management plans, and (7) it requires a standard review of proposed subdivisions, which entails an open-space ordinance design review and a review of criteria. Developers who wish to comply with the ordinance go through a three-step application process, which includes a preapplication conference, preliminary plat review, and final plat review. The County Planning and Zoning Department reviews the plans of all developers who apply.

The ordinance originated when a development in a rural area wanted higher-density zoning without applying to have the area rezoned. Normal zoning permitted 2.5-acre lots, but the developer wanted 1-acre lots. Environmental groups saw this as an opportunity to save land and preserve open space. The ordinance was

(Continued on page 72)

developed to create a voluntary program that allowed smaller lots in exchange for preserving open space.

Current Impact

As of this writing, about fifteen projects that employ this ordinance are under review, and construction has begun on three of them. One of the larger developments currently under construction is Hamlin Grove, a 142.6-acre site with 356 proposed lots. The proposed total amount of open space preserved is about 56 acres.

Pros and Cons

Developers favored the ordinance because it offered the incentive of increased density for preserving open space and it was voluntary. Opposition did come from members of the public who believed that a 25 percent increase in density was too much, and that roads, sewage facilities, and schools could not handle the increase.

Many developers who have applied for density bonuses under this ordinance saw only a 25 percent increase in density and did not understand the environmental factors that go into creating cluster developments that preserve open space. Some did not realize that the open space must be connected, and others believed that golf courses should count as open space. Stormwater management facilities do count as potential open space if the facilities are designed to be functional wildlife habitat. The ordinance also requires that the open space be undivided to the maximum extent possible, and if corridors are used they must be no smaller than 3 acres and have a length-to-width ratio of 4:1.

The Open Space Subdivisions Ordinance allows developers to use different zoning lot sizes without having to go to the board and apply for rezoning. This saves time and lets developers use alternative designs. However, smaller lot sizes are typically an advantage only in developments that have 1-acre or larger lot sizes.

The ordinance can be found at www.municode.com/Resources/gateway .asp?pid=10473&sid=9. Search under: Chapter 62. Land Development Regulations; Article VII. Subdivisions and Plats; Division 5. Open Space Subdivisions.

Source: Adapted from M. Romero and M.E. Hostetler, *Policies That Address Sustainable Site Development*, EDIS circ. 1520 (Gainesville: Wildlife Ecology and Conservation Department, Florida Cooperative Extension Service, Institute of Food and Agricultural Sciences, University of Florida, 2007). Available at http://edis.ifas.ufl.edu/UW254.

Box 12. Harmony Community Development District

A vast open space network exists in the town of Harmony near St. Cloud, Florida. The most innovative feature of this network is Lakeshore Park along Buck Lake (Figure 15). Instead of designing lakefront home lots, the developers chose to create a buffer of wooded wetlands along with a public park. Why would Harmony's developers choose to forgo the potential profits from this incredibly valuable lakefront property? They didn't, and that's the best part.

Because the Florida Statutes permit the creation of community development districts, Harmony formed one to maintain several neighborhood infrastructure projects, such as parks, roads, and right-of-ways. Community development districts are not uncommon in Florida; more than a hundred such districts have been established in the state. One project of Harmony's community development district is the twenty-seven-acre public park along Buck Lake.

A portion of the community development district bond, with a present-day value of $4.7 million, was allocated for the purchase of the land from the developers and will be amortized over a thirty-year period, paid by the owners of the two thousand residential units. The average annual cost for each homeowner for

(Continued on page 74)

Figure 15. Lakeshore Park, Harmony, Florida. Courtesy of Harmony Development Company.

Statutes Web site, www.flsenate.gov/statutes/ (see Title XIII, "Planning and Development," Chapter 190, "Community Development Districts").

4. *Conservation easements:* As discussed in the section about what developers can do, conservation easements may be a useful tool for governments to use to encourage conservation of natural areas on private lands. A landowner can obtain significant monetary savings through tax breaks, or even upfront money, by selling to the city or county the development rights for portions of his or her property. A city or county government could act as a land trust and negotiate conservation easements with landowners. To help spread the word, government agencies should provide educational materials and even organize workshops to promote the use of conservation easements with local land trusts.

5. *Planned unit developments and subdivision regulation:* Planned unit developments entail the development of several parcels of land with different zoning, but in a more flexible way than the underlying zoning. Subdivision regulations govern how one parcel of land is subdivided into smaller parcels for development. Both of these can be structured to address biodiversity conservation. The city of Bellevue, Washington, has a planned unit development regulation that specifically states that 40 percent of the total land area must be designated as open space.[26] Park City, Utah, has a subdivision regulation governing property within certain sensitive areas defined by an overlay zone. The regulation specifies that an applicant must submit a map that delineates sensitive natural areas and

---

the preservation of this land is approximately two hundred dollars per year (paid through homeowners association fees). Harmony's developers reap the benefits of the additional up-front money received by the issuance of capital infrastructure bonds, while the residents of Harmony benefit by having a neighborhood park.

By buffering the lake from upland pollution, maintaining the wildlife habitat, and creating Lakeshore Park as a shared community amenity, Harmony's developers have distributed the value of the lakefront property to all residential units, instead of to a very small group of lakefront homeowners. The shared amenities offered by Buck Lake's wooded wetlands and the planned Lakeshore Park are expected to increase the value of each residential unit by an amount comparable to the annual special assessment fees, thus making habitat preservation benefit the homeowners, the developers, and the wildlife.

wildlife habitat that are located on the property the applicant proposes to develop. Also, the applicant must look for a way to preserve any connections with off-site natural areas.[27]

Although not common, these five growth management strategies have been tried in various localities. However, these strategies often do not adequately address biodiversity conservation. From my experiences, most governments require a *certain percentage* of open space to be set aside, but they do not define it adequately under a regulation. To conserve biodiversity, open space requirements must state that significant natural areas are a priority, and that a secondary priority is to make them as contiguous as possible. It is critical to clearly define open space, because it could be interpreted as golf courses, manicured parks, and other, more industrial uses. In addition, construction and postconstruction issues are not emphasized, and there is no language to address the way nearby subdivisions are built or managed. Below, I offer some strategies that are not typically part of the growth management toolbox for cities and counties, but which should be added to them.

1. *Require or encourage the use of trained contractors.* At a minimum, local policies should require that built environment professionals associated with green development projects be fully trained and aware of practices that promote biodiversity conservation. The policy would state that contractors must have taken a course on how to conserve biodiversity during site construction. Without knowledgeable and engaged contractors, the health of trees and conserved areas is likely to be compromised, and no amount of punitive measures can overcome a lack of understanding of the importance of protecting biodiversity.

2. *Require adequate protection of natural features during construction.* To protect significant trees during the construction phase, policies must address the identification of significant trees and contain stringent regulations concerning proper construction techniques. Construction near conserved areas must be carefully regulated, because careless machine operators may otherwise run through natural areas. The government must have several arborists on staff to oversee construction sites. Stiff fines for improper construction maintenance, and incentives for doing proper construction site management, are ways to encourage sustainable construction techniques. One design recommendation that helps simplify construction management is to preserve groupings of trees instead of protecting only

individual large trees. It is easier to protect a group of trees than many individual ones, and preserving groups of trees creates larger habitat patches and conserves more undisturbed soil.

3. *Require management plans for built and conserved areas.* Some open space policies require a management plan for conserved natural areas, but most do not address the management of neighborhoods within the development. As illustrated throughout this book, residents of such neighborhoods can have a significant impact on conserved areas. An environmental education program that addresses land stewardship on built lots, presented to neighbors, can help to preserve the biological integrity of conserved areas. To help pay for an ongoing education program and management, a policy should require the developer to identify a long-term funding source, such as homeowners association dues.

4. *Create a county, state, or regional biodiversity strategy.* The value of this should not be underestimated, as a well-developed biodiversity strategy can help direct local policies and regulations and offer guidance for public agencies and other stakeholders, such as landowners and developers. While a biodiversity strategy usually comes from a consortium of individuals and public and private agencies, typically such efforts are led by a government agency. A good biodiversity strategy includes strategies and priorities that help to engage private citizens, increase interagency cooperation, and identify financial and policy incentives for conserving and restoring biodiversity. In particular, the strategy must address the design, construction, and management of subdivided land, because these built areas ultimately affect the surrounding natural areas. Subdivisions designed to conserve biodiversity foster a regional biodiversity strategy, one that will engage the built environment community and the public. Washington State has developed a biodiversity strategy and has had several successes (Box 13). There are also international efforts worth mentioning. I spent more than a year in the Canterbury region of New Zealand, where the local government has created a holistic, biodiversity conservation strategy worth looking at (see www.canterburybiodiversity. org.nz). This strategy has twenty-six action items, including such things as helping to provide coordination among stakeholders, identifying key conservation areas, and enhancing public awareness and support. In particular, the strategy has supported and recognized landowner and public efforts to conserve biodiversity.

The ability of governments to encourage the conservation of natural areas is associated with good marketing and education programs. Unfortunately, without marketing, even a good open space policy will be read by few people and ultimately will have little impact. A critical step is to hire a director of biodiversity conservation, one with good public relations skills, who can

---

Box 13. Washington Biodiversity Project

The Washington Biodiversity Conservation Strategy was released in 2007, and it presented this vision statement: "In our lifetimes, the native plants and animals, along with their air, water, and land habitats, are healthy and in harmony with our working landscapes and residential communities. The vital importance of biodiversity conservation is recognized in principle and practice. Washington citizens see themselves as stewards of our natural resources diversity and accept a responsibility to pass the heritage along to their children and future generations in a healthy condition."

This biodiversity project offers a variety of resources and educational components, which can be obtained through its Web site (see www.biodiversity.wa.gov). The strategy has had some significant outcomes, which are currently being used to promote statewide conservation efforts: (1) *It helped define priorities for conservation* by regionally mapping biodiversity value and threats to biodiversity. These maps integrate species and habitat data from multiple sources. (2) *It raised the profile of conservation incentives for landowners.* This ultimately makes biodiversity conservation on working lands and open spaces easy and rewarding. (3) *It engaged citizen scientists* in a program to assist in monitoring Washington's biodiversity. Several BioBlitzes, which are rapid biodiversity inventory projects, have been organized in which citizens partner with scientists. (4) *It made scientific information accessible* to the public. A biodiversity scorecard is under development to help citizens assess and understand biodiversity indicators. (5) *It helped to incorporate biodiversity into local planning efforts,* and this fostered local efforts to incorporate conservation priorities and best practices into planning. (6) *It educated children and adults* through a variety of environmental education programs and media outlets. (7) *It fostered trust, collaboration, and the creation of networks,* helping local communities create solutions.

Source: Adapted from the Washington Biodiversity Project, "Washington Biodiversity Council Achievements, 2005–2009," 2009, www.biodiversity.wa.gov.

communicate with a wide variety of people. Simply placing an open space policy on the books, without having somebody build cooperation among stakeholders, may do little to change current practices. Governments that partner with the private sector and the public facilitate actions on the ground. Each community is different, but here are some steps that will aid in increasing the participation of developers and others in the conservation of trees and natural open space when subdividing land.

- Find a developer motivated to adopt novel design, construction, and postconstruction practices that focus on conserving natural open space and trees. Once the development is completed, the development can be used as a model for spreading the word about conservation practices and government efforts to collaborate with the built environment community. The conservation subdivision would be used to demonstrate local efforts and to communicate with other developers. Developers speaking with one another ultimately promote local participation in biodiversity conservation programs.

- Communicate governmental efforts to conserve urban trees and open space through workshops that target built environment professionals. In particular, invite environmental consulting firms, landowners, contractors, and real estate agents to these workshops. If these individuals are informed and engaged, they ultimately will provide advice and ideas to the developers who hire them.

CHAPTER 4

Improving Community Engagement and Understanding

No matter what has been built, preserved, or landscaped, a community actually conserves biodiversity over the long term only when residents are *engaged*. Studies have indicated that most residents who live in conservation subdivisions do not understand and are not aware of the appropriate management practices for maintaining homes, yards, and neighborhoods in terms of natural resource conservation. A study in Florida found that residents of one conservation subdivision did not differ from, or scored lower than, residents of "conventional" communities on several questions about environmental knowledge, attitudes, and behaviors.[1] In another comparative study, buyers of new homes in conservation subdivisions and conventional communities differed very little from each other in terms of environmental knowledge, attitudes, and behavior. The overall environmental scores were low for all respondents, regardless of community type.[2] Because the impact of surrounding neighborhoods on conserved remnant patches and resident wildlife populations can be large,[3] local residents must understand and value urban wildlife, and recognize how each person's actions can have positive or negative effects on local species.[4]

Green communities are probably not attracting environmentally sensitive residents, and in the absence of an environmental education program to engage residents, a community may engage in environmentally insensitive behaviors rather than manage the community sustainably over the long term. Homeowner understanding and buy-in are essential if the community is to function as a conservation subdivision as originally intended. Although it is the developer who originally implements the conservation design, it is up to the community's residents to manage and maintain many of the sustainable features. Decisions made by homeowners in maintaining their own homes and yards can have drastic consequences for biodiversity.

WHAT CAN RESIDENTS IN A NEIGHBORHOOD DO?

Because biodiversity conservation is ultimately up to each individual resident, the easiest way-to create a neighborhood culture of sustainability is to lead by example. Certain property owners can provide working models of yards and homes that conserve natural resources and promote biodiversity. Home-owners could convert their yards (say, from exotic grass to native plants) or update their homes with water-saving features, such as soil moisture sensors for irrigation, and invite other homeowners over to their property to view and discuss these innovations. Arranging a potluck dinner at the same time would help attract more neighbors. Neighbor-to-neighbor discussions would help demonstrate how converting the yard or adding water-saving features can be done and promote a culture of acceptance. With each new landscaping project, a sign could be installed explaining what has been done and inviting inquiries from neighbors. When just a few people take the first steps to promote natural resource conservation within a neighborhood, other residents begin to take their first steps as well. Research supports the notion that social norms have a huge influence on individual behaviors;[5] in this case, when more and more neighbors conserve biodiversity through actions they take in their yards and homes, the "neighborhood norm" becomes aligned with conserving biodiversity and other natural resources.

The impact on biodiversity can be much greater if several homeowners within a neighborhood decide to design and manage their own lots to incorporate native plants and support native animals. Even neighborhood common areas are affected by individual decisions, and the more that people understand how their own behaviors affect biodiversity, the better these common areas function in terms of habitat for native plants and animals. To get the conversation going, block parties can attract a wide range of neighbors and help to jump-start sustainability efforts in a neighborhood (Figure 16). Videos, TV shows, or radio programs could be used to highlight an urban biodiversity topic and help lay the foundations for a fruitful discussion (Box 14). In my experience, people do not know what the issues are and how to take the

FIGURE 16. Neighbors discussing environmental issues concerning the Kingswood subdivision, Gainesville, Florida. Photo by the author.

Box 14. Having a Conversation with Neighbors

Videos about green landscaping and natural resource conservation can help to get a conversation going. For example, one can view "Landscaping for Wildlife," a half-hour episode of the series *Living Green* (see www.livinggreen.ifas.ufl.edu). Produced by the University of Florida and aired on PBS and local cable stations, *Living Green* addresses an array of sustainable development issues. A group discussion about landscaping for wildlife could be run like a brainstorming session, where all ideas, problems, and solutions are discussed. Concerned neighbors could form a local stewardship committee, facilitating future interaction throughout the neighborhood. One can consider the following questions.

1. What kinds of opportunities exist for landscaping for wildlife in your yard?

Facilitator: Have people list strategies they could employ. Examples include letting portions of yards go wild, removing turf and using native plants, installing rain gardens, and removing invasive exotics.

(Continued on page 82)

first step. Simple networking with local neighbors can help people find local sources of native plants, discuss wildlife-human conflicts, and locate landscaping firms that specialize in natural landscaping. A strong sense of community is an important variable in the creation of sustainable communities, because it leads to an increase in the diffusion of knowledge.[6]

Because some wildlife, such as geese, raccoons, bears, and possums, can become problematic over time, residents must become well informed about the way human actions can create problems between people and certain wildlife species. Of paramount importance is the danger of feeding some wildlife species, either on purpose or inadvertently through outdoor pet dishes and open garbage cans. Feeding may condition them to search for human handouts, or it may artificially increase the number of animals in a neighborhood. It can be dangerous to feed wildlife, especially large animals. In Gatlinburg, Tennessee, nuisance bear problems were partially attributed to people feeding bears to attract tourists.[7] In the case of Canada geese (*Branta* sp.), an overabundance of geese can lead to several environmental problems in neighborhoods.[8] Geese leave an abundance of droppings, leading to the fouling of water bodies, sidewalks, lawns, and open space. They may even become aggressive and attack people and pets. Thus, each homeowner must become aware of the risks of feeding wildlife and take actions to reduce artificial food

---

2. What are the challenges in creating a wildlife-friendly yard? For these challenges, are there solutions?

Facilitator: Have people list the challenges in and solutions to converting a yard. Challenges may include the following: the neighbors may not like it, homeowners association polices may forbid it, homeowners may lack knowledge about removing invasive exotics, and homeowners may not know where to buy native plants. Solutions might include: homeowners can educate their neighbors, meet with the homeowners association, gather literature on invasive exotic plants, and locate native plant nurseries.

3. What kinds of opportunities exist to landscape for wildlife in the neighborhood?

Facilitator: Examples include: homeowners can let their adjacent property boundaries go wild to create larger natural patches; if open spaces are present, they can be restored by installing native plants in them; homeowners can involve the homeowners association in educating the neighborhood; and homeowners can mount neighborhood efforts to remove invasive exotics.

sources so that animals do not become overabundant or lose their natural fear of humans.

WHAT CAN A DEVELOPER DO?

Foremost, a developer can set up an education program. This is a win-win solution, as homeowners have indicated a desire to learn more about local natural history and environmental issues,[9] and an environmental education program can be a marketable feature used by real estate agents to sell a home. To reach a wide range of residents, develop an education program that is both dynamic and visible in the neighborhood. The dynamic aspect of the program allows information to be readily updated. My graduate students and I developed such a program, which consisted of neighborhood signs, a Web site, and a brochure. We collaborated with developers in the town of Harmony, Florida, to implement the program and evaluate its effectiveness. In Harmony, seven signs were placed in areas of high foot traffic, such as sidewalks, trails, and recreational open spaces (Figure 17). An unusual feature of these signs was that each could be taken apart, and new informational panels could be inserted into the viewing area. These dynamic signs allowed a variety of topics to be displayed, and residents could view new information as panels were rotated on a quarterly basis. Associated with these signs, the Web site gave local, more detailed information about various natural resource topics. Harmony's Web site discussed native plants and animals sighted in and around the neighborhoods. One primary advantage of having the Web site, Living in Harmony (www.wec.ufl.edu/extension/gc/harmony/), in addition to the neighborhood signs, was that more information could be displayed and easily be updated, which is done on a fairly regular basis. The third feature of the education program, a brochure, was handed out to new homeowners. The brochure briefly stated the conservation goals for the community and let people know about the signs and the Web site.

It does cost money to build education programs, and funds should be set aside as part of infrastructure costs for the development. Over the long term, funding to manage the education program could be obtained through homeowners association dues. The developer must initiate this and designate that a portion of homeowners association dues will go to maintenance of the education program. That an education program does have a positive impact has been demonstrated by a comparative study showing that homeowners in a neighborhood

FIGURE 17. An educational sign installed along a public path in Harmony, Florida. This and seven other displays were designed to allow for the easy replacement of printed panels: the top frame comes off for insertion of new panels. Photo by Jennifer J. W. Vann.

with an environmental education program consisting of signs, a Web site, and a brochure displayed improved environmental knowledge, attitudes, and behaviors.[10] At the very least, developers should install educational signs throughout the community, because in Harmony the residents obtained more of their environmental information from signs than from a Web site or brochure.[11]

An education delivery system like the one in Harmony is passive. For large, master-planned communities, a developer should be proactive and hire a conservation manager to help educate and engage new homeowners as build-out occurs. Having a local person to run education programs, coordinate conservation activities and events, and solve unforeseen conflicts as the community grows will go a long way toward promoting a culture of sustainability. A large community could take ten, twenty, or even thirty years for all the homes to be built, and a local "go to" manager can help instill stewardship throughout the community.

How to fund a conservation manager and education program? A developer could just build the cost of the program into the overall costs of the development and obtain it from lot sales. Other creative ways could be used, such as selling a portion of the land to a county or city, creating a community development district (see Box 12), and using homeowners association dues. Such costs are an important component of conservation subdivisions, and each developer should make plans to fund education programs.

While an education program may be a good start to the process of informing and motivating residents, other engagement activities may be required to truly establish the sense that environmental practices are the norm within a community. Actual restoration and monitoring projects can catalyze a community to adopt environmental practices, because they are actions visible to the community. Such practices include bird monitoring (e.g., transect counts of birds in the town of Harmony; see www.wec.ufl.edu/extension/gc/harmony/wildlife/birds.htm), water quality monitoring, removal of invasive plants and animals, and planting of native vegetation. With initial help from a developer and perhaps local environmental organizations, a conservation club could be organized to participate in restoration and monitoring projects (Box 15). Such

---

Box 15. Lake Okareka Walkway, Rotorua, New Zealand

Through a collaborative effort between a local landowner, the Environment Bay of Plenty, the Rotorua District Council, Fish and Game New Zealand, and a local Okareka Landcare Group (a volunteer group made up of residents in the area), a walkway near Lake Okareka was built to give residents access to the lakeside (Figure 18). As the walkway was being built, local residents and environmental groups began restoring areas near the lake edge to improve wildlife habitat and increase native plant diversity. Previously, many areas near the lake had been used as pasture right up to the edge of the water, but fences have been installed to keep out cattle. In the past, many people used the area for walks, traversing habitats in the process, and there was concern that these areas were degrading. The boardwalk was designed to keep people on the path, and in some areas the path veers away from the edge of the lake to avoid disturbing waterbirds.

Volunteers from the Lake Okareka Community Association (www.lakeokareka .org/) have taken an interest in the care and management of the lake and the lake edge. Many of the group's activities involve minimizing local impacts and restoring biodiversity to the area, including native planting days and efforts to control introduced predators such as possums and rats. New plantings around the shoreline

(Continued on page 86)

activities create a conservation ethic in a community and aid in disseminating conservation information and practices.

Occasional workshops and presentations by knowledgeable people will help address new and evolving issues and spread the word into surrounding communities. In Madison, Wisconsin, a coalition of city and several nonprofit groups convinced the state not to sell a thirty-one-acre property, and it now contains housing, community gardens, an organic farm, and restored prairie and woodlands (www.troygardens.org). Community GroundWorks, a local nonprofit organization in Madison, manages the property and offers community workshops, trainings, volunteer restoration activities, and nature-based celebrations to involve people in the Madison area. In particular, celebrations with an environmental theme offer opportunities for people to learn about

Figure 18.　A boardwalk built to protect shoreline habitat of Lake Okareka, Rotorua, New Zealand. Photo by Sandra Goodwin.

have buffered the lake from upland pollution and have created habitat for a variety of birds. This is a good example of how a local project can restore habitat and simultaneously create land stewardship within the neighborhood.

natural-resource events. In the town of Harmony, an annual Dark Sky Festival has been highly popular and attracts thousands of people each year to view the stars. It also offers an opportunity to talk about light pollution and the use of full cutoff light fixtures in neighborhoods (see www.wec.ufl.edu/extension/gc/harmony/darksky.htm).

In association with educational activities, a reward system for environmental stewardship could be started by a developer and continued by the neighborhood association. "Yard of the month" or "steward of the month" awards would highlight local efforts by residents, offering opportunities for people to share knowledge. Positive feedback like this would promote environmental stewardship across the neighborhood. Reward systems help engage people and market actions that protect biodiversity.

WHAT CAN A POLICY MAKER DO?

Policies do not exist that address the long-term education and engagement of residents in green communities. As discussed throughout this book, *post-construction issues* are of critical importance, and engaging residents is an important component of long-term management for any community. A policy should encourage or require developers to address long-term management issues and implement a local education program. Because new management issues often arise over time, a government agency should hire a staff member to oversee long-term management issues within residential developments. In particular, this person can help advise developers on the appropriate educational system to install. Each site will have its own natural resource issues that must be addressed on built lots and conserved areas. Although the developer will probably hire an environmental consultant to develop and install an education program, quality control is necessary. A developer could choose to install static, cheap plastic signs that provide little information. Developing a program that truly engages homeowners and contains the appropriate information to permit people to take action actually requires a good deal of planning and investigation. One of the first steps of a good environmental education program is the identification of *barriers* to sustainable behaviors and of ways to remove them.[12] Identifying barriers takes some research, and once the barriers are identified, then appropriate solutions could be offered. For example, advice on how to use native plants is useless if residents do not know where to find native plants. Locating sources of native plants and informing residents of where to purchase them are important steps in fostering behavioral changes.

As mentioned earlier, governments should take part in reviewing neighborhood education programs. This oversight could be a collaboration between local academic institutions, private entities, and nongovernmental organizations. Of course, such oversight takes funding, and development impact fees constitute one mechanism to raise funds. Municipalities use impact fees to

---

Box 16. BioBlitz, Connecticut Style

The Center for Conservation and Biodiversity, the University of Connecticut, and the Connecticut State Museum of Natural History organized annual BioBlitzes between 1999 and 2009 (http://web2.uconn.edu/mnh/bioblitz/). During a BioBlitz, scientists and members of the public would gather together for a twenty-four-hour survey of organisms in a specified location. The public would get to observe the scientists' activities, interact with the scientists, and participate in a range of educational activities presented by several nature-based organizations. In 2009, the BioBlitz brought together citizens and educators to observe and identify species in Keney Park, a 693-acre park in Hartford. Many individuals, sponsors, and public and private groups collaborated to host the event. Scientists from the University of Connecticut and Goodwin College helped to collect and identify specimens. The city councils of Hartford and East Hartford and other groups organized and advertised the event.

As a result of the 2009 inventories, approximately 1,715 species of various taxa were found, including mammals, birds, plants, fish, insects, and fungi. The BioBlitz helped to direct awareness to several rare habitats and species within the park. And the event yielded one new state sighting of a species: a rare owlet moth (*Ufeus plicatus*). Surrounding some little bluestem grasslands and a stand of pitch pine, several open sandy areas housed some rare species. The open sand patches in particular had a large population of the big sand tiger beetle (*Cicindela formosa*), which appears on the state list of threatened species, and the endangered ghost dune tiger beetle (*Cicindela lepida*). The population of big sand tiger beetles is thought to be one of the largest in Connecticut. The BioBlitzes in Connecticut were a celebration of biodiversity found in metropolitan areas. They raised awareness of urban biodiversity across a city, generated a bit of data, and provided a forum for kids and adults alike to connect with their natural heritage.

---

raise funds for open space or for meeting community recreational needs; such fees could be used to hire personnel to help oversee neighborhood education programs, concurrently addressing barriers in neighborhoods where residents try to implement local environmental actions.

Engaging the public is essential, and governments should play a major role in spreading the word about managing homes, yards, and neighborhoods for biodiversity. In addition to undertaking general public outreach efforts, governments could target engagement activities for certain neighborhoods. The activities could take the form of a BioBlitz, like the ones organized by the University of Connecticut. These rapid inventories of animals, plants, and habitats are designed to increase people's awareness of the diversity of life in their immediate neighborhoods (Box 16). Often in partnership with scientists and local education institutions, citizens participating in a BioBlitz conduct twenty-four-hour surveys to list the variety of species found within a designated area. These areas could be nearby parks or even front and backyards. In addition, governments could organize celebrations, workshops, and seminars that tout the benefits of biodiversity conservation and highlight plants and animals found in cities. These activities raise public awareness and create a grassroots network of concerned individuals that fosters local stewards and biodiversity champions.

CHAPTER 5

Landscaping and Individual Lots

Built lots, cumulatively, take up a large portion of a subdivision. Even if a sub-division has conserved natural areas, the sum of activities in each individual yard can dramatically affect these conserved areas and reduce biological diversity. Yard designs and management can also affect natural areas miles away from residential developments, by means of such things as nutrient runoff and the escape of invasive plants installed in yards. Water runoff can carry large loads of pollutants into streams that ultimately transport these nutrients to other water bodies. Invasive exotic berries originating with landscape plants are eaten by birds, and the seeds are deposited in natural areas. While the potential for harm is great, opportunities exist to create native landscapes that can support a wide variety of indigenous plants and animals. If enough people create native backyards, then a neighborhood could house a number of different native wildlife species and a variety of native plants. The first step, though, is a major shift in the design of conventional yards—the reduction of lawn.

REDUCING THE LAWN

Reducing the amount of turfgrass in a neighborhood and city is probably the most significant action people can take to conserve biodiversity. However, lawn care is a common topic discussed among neighbors, and lawn care is a huge industry. From fertilizers to lawnmowers, a multitude of products have been developed to keep lawns perfect and green. Lawn care is a cultural pastime, and a green lawn is status symbol and sometimes a competitive enterprise.

Lawns and the upkeep of lawns are part of American, Canadian, and European traditions: people spend billions of dollars and millions of hours on them. Everyday, people are bombarded with messages about how to best take care of their lawns. Homeowners agonize when their lawns turn brown or weeds start to pop up. That lawns are beloved is reflected in the number of ordinances and laws addressing how lawns should look. People can get bent out of shape if their neighbor's lawn does not conform to the perceived norm.[1]

People are familiar with the manicured yard, but not the natural yard. Landscaping techniques can make even natural yards aesthetically pleasing to the human eye, but first one has to take a step to envision what the property would look like with a minimal amount of lawn. The following pages outline the pros of giving up the lawn, and the cons of maintaining the lawn. Before I address what residents, developers, and policy makers can do, it will be useful to consider a brief history of where the idea of the lawn came from and why it is somewhat ingrained in the psyche of urban dwellers.

A BRIEF HISTORY OF THE LAWN

The public's fascination with lawns probably stems from both nature and nurture. Humans, having evolved in the east African Rift Valley, have been exposed to savannah landscapes for a very long time. Savannah landscapes are typified by short grasses and a scattering of large trees, and the long evolutionary trek in Africa may have left a permanent preference for this type of landscape in the human psyche. In other words, human genetic memory may be biased toward savannah landscapes. Researchers have done studies that indicate that all sorts of people of different nationalities and ages prefer savannah landscapes.[2] Thus, the proliferation of the modern-day lawns may be partly a result of this human predisposition.

Current environmental and social factors also influence human behavior. Our society may prefer savannah landscapes, but the art of designing and managing lawns is a recent cultural phenomenon. The concept of the maintained lawn seems to have originated in western Europe, especially in France and England, in the eighteenth century.

But what started the Europeans on lawns? Interest in the lawn probably began with humans' overwhelming desire to control and contain nature. Nature seemed (especially back then) like such an overriding force that the ability to contain it and shape it was regarded as a sign of wealth and prestige.

One of the earliest steps that eventually led to the production of lawns was the practice of gardening. During medieval times, ornamental gardens were created to provide a place for entertaining, dancing, romance, and peaceful solitude. Herbal, vegetable, and fruit gardens were also created to provide essential foods and herbs. The construction of gardens became an art form, and set a precedent for present-day manicured landscapes.[3]

As people gained more resources and made technological advances, formal gardens soon gave rise to another art form—the lawn. Lawns that were cropped short not only permitted an unobstructed view of the landscape around them but also nicely set off the gardens created by the homeowners. Some of the earliest designers of lawns were English. One famous English landscape designer, Lancelot "Capability" Brown (nicknamed "Capability" because he always talked about the capability of a piece of property), brought the concept of the manicured lawn to mainstream English society. Brown's landscapes were expansive, and most of the vegetation was removed to make room for the lawn. His landscapes instilled in English society a desire to have lawns all across the country. Maintaining these lawns was labor intensive. To cut them, people used scythes and even sheep or cows! Despite the maintenance requirements, Brown's landscapes became a status symbol for people throughout Europe.

Climate had a lot to do with the success of lawns in English landscapes. England's mild climate and its abundant rainfall allowed grass to flourish. Lawns do not work so well in other environments around the globe. Nonetheless, the concept of the lawn was popularized in other parts of the world—even regions that lacked the proper environment for them. When the British colonized new areas such as Africa, Australia, and North America, they brought along special varieties of European grass seed and introduced the English lawn. European transplants also included (usually by accident) a wide variety of weedy species, such as European dandelions.

In the United States, the idea of the lawn did not really take hold among the general public until after the Civil War. Large lawns were first attempted by rich landowners who viewed English lawns as something to which to aspire. Many, such as Thomas Jefferson at Monticello and George Washington at Mount Vernon, sculpted their landscapes with vast swaths of lawns. The general populace, too, admired these lawns, and even today people come from miles around to view Monticello and Mount Vernon. Many famous and wealthy individuals wanted to see the "scruffy" American landscape become tamed, and they strove to have lawns on their own properties. The "greening" of America had begun.[4]

When people began to own their own homes and property, little "Monticellos" began to appear everywhere. As the industrial revolution developed in America, more and more people began to live in cities. By the early 1800s, cities became unpleasant and were viewed as unhealthy places in which to live. Wealthy people who moved out of the cities built small individual homes, and the suburbs were born. However, lawns still did not catch on right away. Managing a lawn was time-consuming and difficult, and one would have to take care of a lot of farm animals or hire workers to laboriously hack at the rapidly growing grass.

During most of the 1800s, only a few, rich landowners in the United States had the time and the resources to maintain a lawn. The single most important event that changed everything was the invention of the mechanical lawnmower. An Englishman by the name of Edwin Budding invented the lawnmower in the 1830s. This invention eventually allowed almost everybody to have a cropped landscape. Cows and sheep were replaced by this mechanical animal, and lawns became a common feature in English yards. In North America, lawns became mainstream by the late 1800s. As the lawnmower improved over the years, millions of property owners could, by themselves, mow their lawns.

Climate, though, was a problem for North American homeowners. The amount of rainfall was not adequate for most homeowners to maintain a healthy lawn, and it was difficult to manually provide water throughout the yard. But necessity prompted another invention, and in 1871, J. Lessler of Buffalo, New York, invented the water sprinkler., a contraption that allowed property owners to easily water their lawns. With a water sprinkler, whether the proper amount of rainfall occurred or not became inconsequential. All homeowners with access to water could now keep a nice green lawn, even in arid regions such as Arizona.

The concept of the American lawn began in Europe; how did lawn maintenance become such a passion in today's culture? According to Virginia Stenkins, author of *The Lawn: A History of an American Obsession*,[5] three large organizations did much to popularize lawns: the United States Golf Association, the United States Department of Agriculture, and the Garden Club of America. It was a three-pronged approach. The agricultural revolution, along with the growing popularity of golf, fueled the work of many researchers who were attempting to develop turf varieties that could grow in different climates and soils. Decades of research have produced a wide variety of grasses, which has made it easy for any homeowner to grow a lawn. The Department of Agriculture and the Golf Association funded a lot of this research, but it was really the Garden Club of America that spread the word about turf. Garden clubs existed in every city and neighborhood throughout North America, and they all glorified the beauty and necessity of a well-maintained lawn. The perfect lawn, free of insects and weeds, became a status symbol.

Lawns in urban and suburban landscapes are a dominant feature in many areas around the world. Almost every yard contains some amount of turfgrass. Unfortunately, the maintenance of lawns has environmental consequences for both local and global environments. Of note, lawn maintenance is connected to global climate change.

LAWNS CONTRIBUTE TO GLOBAL CLIMATE CHANGE

Global climate change is a result of the earth's atmospheric temperature getting hotter than what has been experienced in recent history. The earth's surface temperature has been shown to have gradually increased, and scientists predict that this will have disastrous consequences across the planet.[6] If the temperature gets hot enough, a significant portion of the polar ice caps will melt, which will cause a rise in the oceans, flooding beachfront areas in many coastal states. Also, a rise in temperature will dramatically change global climatic patterns, making it wetter in some areas and drier in others. The location of vegetation around the world will change dramatically, too. For example, the conifer forest line will begin to shift north. This means that, eventually, some national parks, including Yellowstone National Park, will lose most of their coniferous trees, which are more adapted to cooler climates. In the southern United States, areas will become much hotter on average, especially affecting people living in cities and agriculture.

The cause of global climate change is a change in the earth's atmosphere. The sun heats up the earth when intense light rays strike the earth. The earth and its inhabitants absorb only a small amount of these rays; most of the sunlight is reflected off the earth's surface, back toward space. However, not all of this sunlight escapes into space; a portion of the light, in the form of heat, is retained, because certain atmospheric gases reflect heat back down onto the earth. Carbon dioxide (CO_2), methane, nitrous oxide, and ozone are four gases known to reflect heat back down to earth. These gases are an important part of the atmosphere, because without them, this planet would be very cold. These gases, also called "greenhouse gases," act like the glass in a greenhouse, trapping some of the heat and making the earth's surface a comfortable place for plants and animals to live. But while these gases are necessary for a comfortable environment, when their volume in the atmosphere grows too high, the earth heats up more than usual. It is like increasing the thickness of the glass in a greenhouse: the thicker the glass, the more heat is trapped inside.

Scientists have reached a consensus on this topic, stating that, although the earth's temperature has fluctuated over many of thousands of years, this current rise in temperature is due, in part, to human activity, and that humans must reduce greenhouse gas emissions.[7] Although greenhouse gases occur naturally in the atmosphere, the huge number of people on earth, with their need for fuel, has resulted in the production of excess quantities of these gases. The primary source of this excess is the consumption of fossil fuels, which are drawn from beneath the earth's surface. The burning of coal and oil releases vast quantities of CO_2 into the atmosphere. Driving cars, burning coal for electricity, and yes, even mowing lawns (the lawnmower needs fuel to operate), all contribute to the vast amount of CO_2 being released.

Many different types of organisms absorb and store CO_2. Photosynthetic organisms utilize carbon dioxide to survive and grow. Plants of all types, including algae and small microorganisms such as phytoplankton, use CO_2 to live, grow, and reproduce. Generally, their combined effect takes enough CO_2 out of the atmosphere that it does not build up. However, with humans producing an abundance of CO_2, this gas has accumulated in the atmosphere much faster than it has been absorbed, and global warming is occurring.

In urban landscapes, the production and upkeep of lawns contribute to global warming. The act of producing sod affects the ability of the land to sequester carbon. Land cleared to make way for sod farms removes the very trees and other plants that take up CO_2. Plus, it takes a good deal of energy to harvest and ship sod to cities (consuming more fuel of course). Maintaining installed turf, through irrigation, fertilization, and mowing, consumes a lot of energy, which translates to the emission of more CO_2. Highly maintained urban turf, with its associated fertilization, irrigation, and mowing regimes, is responsible for more CO_2 than the turfgrass can sequester.[8] In addition, urban turfgrass typically emits nitrous oxide after fertilization. Nitrous oxide has a much worse global warming potential, as its heat-absorbing potential is approximately *three hundred times* greater than that of CO_2. Urban greenspace made up primarily of turfgrass is actually a source of CO_2 rather than a sink.[9] Removing lawn and replacing it with native vegetation enhances biodiversity and the ability of neighborhoods to offset carbon emissions and reduce the total carbon footprint of a city.

WHAT CAN RESIDENTS IN A NEIGHBORHOOD DO?

Install Native Plants

Installing natives usually requires the reduction of the amount of lawn. Lawn is like concrete to most species of animals, because it offers little food or cover. Installing native plants increases the diversity of the area's plant cover, and the indigenous vegetation provides habitat for animals. Landscaping with native plants provides better food and cover for native wildlife than landscaping with nonnative plants. The diversity of native urban birds increases with native vegetation,[10] more native plants serve as host plants for butterfly larvae,[11] and the diversity of native bees increases with the occurrence of native plants.[12]

Natives also require less care and resources, such as water, fertilizers, and pesticides, to maintain than exotic plants. Using less water, fertilizers, and pesticides ultimately means less impact on local and surrounding natural areas. Many states have native plant societies, which offer local information about native plants (www.plantsocieties.org). Information on where to purchase native plants can be found at PlantNative, a national native plant nurseries clearinghouse (www.plantnative.com/). Posted at its Web site is a "how to naturescape" document that helps homeowners incorporate natives into their landscapes and offers tips on landscaping to attract wildlife.

Remove Invasive Exotics

An invasive exotic species is an introduced species that has been shown to displace the native vegetation. An "exotic" is any organism that exists in an area where it historically did not occur, usually having been introduced by humans. "Invasive" species are those that form self-sustaining and expanding populations within areas, displacing native plants and associated wildlife. They can also alter natural processes such as fire and water flow. For example, the submersed introduced water plant called hydrilla (*Hydrilla verticillata*) clogs waterways in the South.

Thus, an invasive exotic species comes from somewhere else and is prolific in the area where it has been introduced. Thousands of new plants and animals have been introduced into North America. Some have become established and are considered invasive. Why do some plants and animals become invasive in certain areas? In general, invasive species are adapted to a particular climate and thrive in new areas with similar conditions. They can easily grow and reproduce because they are free from the stresses of their natural predators, parasites, and diseases that kept them in check in their native habitat. If they reach high numbers in the wild, they outcompete native plants and animals for food and space, and some natives can become locally extinct.

There is a long history of introduced plant and animal species in North America. They have arrived in a number of different ways, and many got their start here unintentionally. Many invasive plants came by way of the ornamental plant trade—some were planted in urban and rural areas before scientists knew they could spread. Coral ardesia (*Ardisia crenata*), for example, is an invasive exotic shrub with red berries that has escaped from yards into natural systems. The plant is used as an ornamental in urban landscapes, and the berries are transported into natural areas by water and even birds. Kudzu (*Puereria trilobata*) was originally planted in the early 1920s to control soil erosion along the banks of ditches and to serve as forage for farm animals. It has since taken over vast areas in the southeastern states and is difficult to control. Certain construction practices help to spread invasive exotic plants. Land clearing favors many invasive plant species because they are adapted to disturbances and are the first to invade a construction site.

Invasive exotic plants often spread into an area and outcompete the native plants that wildlife species depend on for food or shelter. For example, Australian pine trees (*Casuarina equisetifolia*) quickly colonize disturbed beaches, and so prevent the establishment of native plant species. These invaders produce a dense layer of dead leaves and branches beneath the trees and smother most herbaceous vegetation. One study found that small mammal populations are less dense in Australian pine habitat compared to native forest communities.[13] Invasive exotic plants also affect native plant and wildlife populations by altering ecological processes. Burma reed (*Neyraudia reynaudiana*), a tall grass from Asia, is a good example. This highly flammable invasive exotic promotes more frequent fires and causes an abnormally high mortality of native vegetation.[14]

Many invasions of exotic animals found in the environment originated with the release of pets. Examples include Burmese pythons (*Python molurus bivittatus*), Nile monitor lizards (*Varanus niloticus*), and cane toads (*Bufo marinus*), which are thriving in the wild in several states in the South. All of these animals can be purchased in pet stores. People have intentionally or unintentionally released such pets, and if they become abundant these animals prey on native wildlife and outcompete them in the effort to find food and space. Other species, such as the European starling (*Sturnus vulgaris*), have been released into the wild to create viable populations for people to enjoy; still others, such as the Cuban tree frog (*Osteopilus septentrionalis*), have been released by accident through trade. European starlings are fierce competitors for nesting cavities in urban areas and are known to evict woodpeckers and other native birds from nests.[15] Cuban tree frogs, which are large, eat many native tree frog species.[16]

It is of primary importance to not release exotic pets under any circumstances and to not plant invasive vegetation in a yard. A national list of invasive exotic plant and animal species can be found at the National Invasive Species Information Center (www.invasivespeciesinfo.gov/). Further, people in every neighborhood should learn to identify invasive species and discover techniques for getting rid of them.

Keep Cats Indoors and Dogs on a Leash

Cats kill millions of birds each year,[17] and they are one of several significant factors that affect bird populations. Cats are prolific hunters, and the sheer number of cats roaming the yards in residential areas takes a toll on local birds and other animals. Here are some suggestions to help protect wildlife from cats. First and foremost, keep cats indoors at all times. Not only is this healthy for birds, but it is healthy for cats too. Many cats get injured in fights with other cats, or are exposed to deadly diseases when they come in contact with other animals. More information about keeping cats indoors is available from the Cats Indoors Campaign at the American Bird Conservancy, www .abcbirds.org.

Cats that do go outside should be let out after 10 A.M. Birds usually feed intensely in the morning and are not as wary of cats at that time. Attaching a bell to a cat can work because the ringing alerts the birds—although, I have seen some cats adapt and move without creating a sound, until it is too late for the bird. A somewhat new product for eliminating predation by cats is a bib that prevents them from pouncing on and catching animals. One study showed that the bib prevented 81 percent of the cats tested from catching birds.[18]

Increase Vertical Layering and Keep Snags

Increasing plant structure between the ground and the tree canopy is called "vertical layering." Planting bushes or ground covers below trees increases the vertical layers in a yard. Layers in a landscape give more cover and feeding opportunities to wildlife. Not only does vertical layering provide additional wildlife habitat, but it also increases the diversity of the plants. Ultimately, using native vegetation increases biodiversity simply because more species of plants occupy the landscape. Keeping dead trees, called snags, on a property also benefits a variety of organisms (Box 17). Many wildlife species use snags for feeding and nesting, but dead trees are often in short supply in urban areas.[19] If safety is a concern in leaving snags standing, then one can cut part of the tree, leaving it about fifteen feet tall. This will still be valuable to wildlife.

Box 17. The Case for Snags

What is a snag? Essentially it is a dead, upright tree. Snags are in short supply in urban neighborhoods, however, because many are removed. Snags provide habitat for a wide range of beetles and other insects, which are in turn food for birds. Snags are also used for communication: many woodpeckers pound trees to attract mates and let rivals know the location of their territory.

Furthermore, many species of birds shelter in the cavities or tree holes found on snags. Some cavity-nesting birds are *primary* cavity-nesters and some are *secondary* cavity-nesters. Primary cavity-nesters, such as woodpeckers, excavate their own cavities, usually in dead or dying trees. In fact, snags are correlated to the abundance and distribution of a variety of urban woodpeckers in urban areas. Secondary cavity-nesters, such as bluebirds, chickadees, owls, great-crested flycatchers, and so on, don't make their own cavities but use cavities excavated by primary cavity-nesting birds, or they use natural cavities. Thus, retaining snags on a property benefits a wide variety of species by presenting them with foraging and nesting opportunities. Where snags are in short supply, bird boxes could be installed. Secondary cavity-nesting birds are the species most likely to use artificial bird boxes, whereas woodpeckers do not often use nest boxes.

Source: C.M. Blewett and J.M. Marzluff, "Effects of urban sprawl on snags and the abundance and productivity of cavity-nesting birds," *Condor* 107(3) (2005): 678–93.

For areas without a dead or dying tree, importing a small snag is an option. One could obtain permission to remove any downed trees from a property. These snags could be planted in the yard.

Increasing vertical structure can attract more birds. People love birds—their melodious songs and antics provide homeowners with a touch of nature in the comfort of their own homes. Many people find solace in watching birds and other wildlife in their backyards, and millions have purchased bird feeders to attract birds. Cardinals, sparrows, mourning doves, house finches, robins, and blue jays are commonly seen in backyards, but to attract songbirds like the colorful neotropical migrants (e.g., the American redstart, *Setophaga ruticilla*), one has to create a habitat that mimics the birds' native habitats.

Getting rid of lawn is the first step. In the bird world, lawns tend to attract certain species that are adapted to feeding in grass, such as starlings and robins, but a majority of the birds do not forage in lawns. Because urban turf is an exotic monoculture, it tends to have limited insect, fruit, and flower diversity. Only a few species of birds can actually eat grass or forage for insects just beneath the surface of lawns. And lawns do not provide hiding places in which birds can raise families. Cats, dogs, and other urban predators would quickly discover a bird nest located in the middle of a lawn. All species of birds look for habitat that provides not only food but also nesting sites that are somewhat protected from predators.

The best way to attract more bird species is to add natural vegetation to a yard. Urban areas that have a large amount of native vegetation attract a greater diversity of birds,[20] because native birds are adapted to local plants. Even the conservation of trees and the associated canopy can improve the diversity and number of birds found in urban areas.[21] One of the easiest ways to increase the local birdlife is to just stop mowing portions of a yard. Depending on the location of the yard, a variety of beautiful flowers and other plants will come up. Mowing essentially favors grasses, as they are adapted to having the tops cut off, and most other herbaceous plants are not adapted to having the tops cut off. Birds feed on a variety of native plants, consuming fruits and other parts of the plant, and sometimes feeding on insects and other critters that hide in the vegetation. Hummingbirds sip nectar from flowers, thrushes and mockingbirds consume fruit, and some of the more carnivorous feathered friends, such as hawks, feed on the small animals that may lurk in the vegetation. A large number of birds are insectivorous, consuming a wide variety of insects. Birds have specific bodily features, such as beak shape, as well as specific behavioral characteristics, that are designed primarily for hunting, catching, and consuming of insects. A diversity of plants means a diversity of insects, which translates into a diversity of birds.

Reducing turfgrass and maintaining native vegetation will attract a greater variety of insects and other arthropods (animals with external skeletons), including beetles, moths, butterflies, and spiders and other arachnids. Spiders play an important role, as many bird species feed on spiders (protein from these small critters is an important nutrient for baby birds), and some, such as hummingbirds, even use spiderweb to construct delicate nests. Interestingly, to help their nestlings grow, hummingbirds primarily feed their young insects and spiders instead of nectar. With the increase of insects in a backyard (especially the flying ones), spiders have a sufficient food source to make it worthwhile to spin webs. With more spiders and webs around, more birds will come into a backyard to eat and perhaps even build nests.

To attract larger bird species, larger patches of natural vegetation must be created. In most cases, one yard is not big enough to attract some species—a grouping of a few trees may not provide enough cover. Neighbors can agree to allow adjoining properties to go native, providing enough cover to attract species that require large patches of habitat. Also, a neighborhood association can create a local initiative to plant native vegetation in common spaces, which would dramatically increase the diversity of birds that visit people's homes in a neighborhood. Neighborhood conservation groups could go around the neighborhood and identify and remove invasive exotic plants, limiting the spread of these problematic species.

For lawn that remains, one should reduce or eliminate all fertilizer, herbicide, and pesticide applications to minimize the impact of runoff on the surrounding natural habitat. If fertilizer is necessary, organic, slow-release fertilizers are good options. Also, one should avoid having a monoculture of grass. Lawns that are mixed with herbs and other plants are much more diverse than a carpet of grass. Let me digress for a moment and focus on what the word *weed* means. The word is not a specific botanical term. *Weed* simply describes a plant that is not wanted. Thorny rose bushes in a meadow would not be desirable to a farmer, and he or she might designate these rose bushes as "weeds" and try to eradicate them. In urban yards, various herbs have been deemed weeds by most people because they want a carpet of grass devoid of other plants. These plants may actually be native plants, and allowing them to coexist with the grass will promote biodiversity.

Help Reduce Greenhouse Gases and Save Money

A sure way to increase the amount of CO_2 sequestered by a yard is to reduce the amount of space allocated to turfgrass and to increase the amount of natural vegetation that does not require mowing or fertilization. Collectively, neighborhoods that reduce the amount of mowed lawn and increase the amount of natural vegetation are not only taking up more CO_2 but also decreasing pollution of the environment. The pollution created by a gas-powered mower in one year is equivalent to a car driving fourteen thousand miles.[22] When mowing the lawn, one should avoid gasoline-driven mowers. Using a push-type reel mower neither consumes fuel nor pollutes the environment. Reducing the area that requires lawn maintenance also saves money. Large amounts of money are spent on lawns and landscaped areas each year. According to a 1998 California report,[23] the average homeowner spends about $310 per year; collectively, Californians spend $9.7 billion dollars annually for lawn and landscaping maintenance, including the maintenance of schools and parks. The cost and upkeep of gasoline lawnmowers, leaf blowers, and weed whackers can be high. Fertilizers, pesticides, and herbicides are also costly. Moreover, time is money. The figures I've mentioned do not account for how much time people spend maintaining a lawn.

WHAT CAN A DEVELOPER DO?

Landscape architects often determine the designs of the lots; developers should hire only landscape architects and landscaping companies who know how to install and maintain natural landscapes. The hired landscape architect should have a good knowledge of which plants work the best in a locality. While a yard could contain a number of native plants, a poor design with natives can result in a maintenance nightmare for homeowners. Following are two common mistakes made by landscape architects and designers.[24]

Mistake no. 1: Overplanting. Small trees and shrubs are often planted too close together in order to create a "full" look. The result several years later is a crowded landscape. When a yard is overplanted, mature plants must be removed or drastically pruned to reduce competition.

Solution: An "instant landscape" is often not the best technique for natural yards. The landscape architect should account for the mature size of plants and give them room and time to grow. Homeowners should be educated about how long natural landscaping will take to mature and fill in.

Mistake no. 2: Cluttering Lawn Areas with Trees and Shrubs. Plants scattered throughout a lawn appear unorganized. They also create maintenance problems in terms of mowing, raking, and giving plants the amount of water they need.

Solution: One should group shrubs and trees in mulched plant beds and avoid installing narrow strips of turfgrass. Narrow areas of lawn are difficult to water appropriately and maintain. Having grouped areas of lawn and landscaped beds allows one to install an irrigation system that can deliver the appropriate amount of water to each plant type.

Developers have control over the type of landscaping installed in finished lots and shared areas. The most important action a developer can take is to limit the amount of lawn and to use native plants as much as possible. As stated before, limiting the use of exotic plants goes a long way toward promoting local biodiversity. When built lots are installed with native landscaping, it sets up a social norm in which people become local stewards of their own yards as well as nearby natural areas (Box 18). Without native landscaping and other conservation features in place, no reinforcement takes place, and sometimes the message of natural resource conservation gets lost. The maintenance of yards made up primarily of turfgrass and exotics typically takes more water, pesticides, and fertilizers, and may affect nearby conservation areas through runoff.

Typically, developers sell lots to individual builders, and they subsequently build the homes and landscape the sites. It is important to select builders who support the goal of biodiversity conservation, but developers should also create a set of guidelines governing how lots are developed. These guidelines would contain principles of biodiversity conservation, and the purpose would be to conserve biodiversity to the fullest extent possible. The document should state that native landscaping is preferred, and it should contain a list of native plants appropriate for the region. All landscape and construction plans should be submitted to a knowledgeable landscape review committee that knows about, and supports, biodiversity conservation. This way, negotiations between the review committee and the builder can produce a solution that will conserve or restore biodiversity within each yard. A landscape review committee can consist of landscape architects and environmental consultants that the developer used in the original design of the community.

Topsoil conservation, keeping the natural topography, and conserving significant native trees and vegetation should be top priorities stated in the guidelines. This involves narrowing construction activities to the footprint of the building itself and leaving the rest of the lot alone. A technique to keep construction within the footprint of a building is to use *stem wall construction* (Figure 20). This technique minimizes site grading and preserves existing vegetation and soil, because the construction zone is kept small. Without stem wall construction, fill dirt is often required to raise the grade of the lot to meet flood requirements, and fill dirt may have to be used across the entire lot. However, if one uses stem wall construction, only the footprint of the home is raised up the required amount to meet flood standards. This way, the lots do not have to be entirely graded; the topsoil and native vegetation are conserved on a lot-by-lot basis. Conserving soil is a critical step, because landscaped plants and turf installed in conserved soil have a much better chance of surviving than plants installed in fill dirt. Plants need less fertilizer and water

---

Box 18. Prairie Crossing Development, Illinois

Prairie Crossing is a 677-acre conservation community situated about an hour west of Chicago. A mixture of single-family homes and condominiums, the subdivision incorporates many natural features in landscaped lots and open space. More than 60 percent of the site is protected land containing farm fields, pastures, lakes, native prairies, and wetlands. In particular, homeowners are required to plant at least 20 percent of every landscaped yard with prairie plants (Figure 19). This rule raised homeowners' awareness of native prairie grassland, and many homeowners increased the amount of prairie plants in their yards beyond the required 20 percent.

A study that compared the land ethic of people who visited the Prairie Learning Center at the Neil Smith National Wildlife Refuge, in neighboring Iowa, and of people who had yards with native prairie plantings in Prairie Crossing, revealed a notable difference between the two groups. While participants learned something at the center about native prairie ecology, few expressed an interest in changing their own yard management practices. Most of the participants considered prairies to be part of the region's natural heritage, apart from built environments. In contrast, Prairie Crossing residents were increasing the number of native prairie plants in their landscapes and discussing ways to minimize the amount of nutrients that would enter the lake. Thus, this one act of incorporating native landscaping in individual lots went a long way to help people understand the connections between built and natural environments and to promote land stewardship.

if the soil has high percentage of organic matter. Fill dirt is sterile, with little or no organic matter, and plants in this environment need excessive amounts of water and fertilizer to become established. Keeping plants alive in fill dirt means more water and energy consumed, and there is a risk that much of the applied fertilizer will run off and affect natural areas. On smaller lots it is more difficult to avoid soil compaction across the entire lot, but using stem wall construction reduces the amount of fill dirt needed. If done correctly, homes will be tucked within the natural vegetation, and only a minimal amount of fill dirt will be needed around the construction pad of each house.

Another aspect developers and builders have control over is the model home. Typically, model homes are constructed and used to promote sales of future lots and homes. The yards around these model homes should contain

Figure 19. In the community of Prairie Crossing, Illinois, lots are landscaped with native prairie plants. Photo by Vicky Ranney.

Source: R.H. Thompson, "Overcoming barriers to ecologically sensitive land management: Conservation subdivisions, green developments, and the development of a land ethic," *Journal of Planning Education and Research* 24(2) (2004): 141–153.

FIGURE 20. Stem wall construction for a residential home. The floor of the house is raised to meet flooding standards, which means less fill dirt and grading will be necessary on the lot. This technique promotes the conservation of topsoil and natural vegetation; note the conserved trees in the background. Courtesy of Program for Resource Efficient Communities.

native landscaping and reduced turfgrass areas. Such model homes and landscapes will set the tone for the community and educate potential homeowners. All the sales staff must be educated about the environmental features within and around a model home and able to discuss them with homebuyers.

Developers should implement an education program that communicates how to plant and maintain a landscape with biodiversity in mind; neighborhood signs and a Web site are a visible way to do this (for an example, see www .wec.ufl.edu/extension/gc/harmony/landscaping.htm). The education program addresses postconstruction engagement of residents, but of equal importance is what happens during construction. Having trained contractors, civil engineers, and landscape architects is critical. Protecting large trees, conserving soil, and using native landscaping plants on the lots should be priorities. The way trees are installed is one of the biggest predictors of the long-term survival of healthy plant communities. Developers must hire designers and landscaping companies with a proven track record. If a company does subcontract the planting responsibilities, it should have proof that the subcontractors are trained as well. An interview over the phone or in person can establish whether sustainable landscaping practices are at the core of their businesses.

Even with good lot designs that incorporate the concepts of biodiversity conservation, developers need to establish rules and guidelines for long-term yard maintenance that emphasize biodiversity conservation and environmental maintenance. For new communities, this can be done through the development of community covenants, conditions, and restrictions that explicitly state environmental landscaping practices. At a minimum, the covenants, conditions, and restrictions should allow homeowners to convert their lawns to native landscaping and should contain information about recommended native plantings to use. The best long-term solution would be to hire one landscaping company who will use environmentally sound practices to maintain all the lots and open spaces within a community. This would provide more consistent maintenance than would occur if maintenance were to be left to individual homeowners.

WHAT CAN A POLICY MAKER DO?

Incentive-based or regulatory policies can be crafted to encourage sustainable landscape designs and management strategies (see examples of sustainable-landscaping policies at http://edis.ifas.ufl.edu/uw253). Native-plant ordinances could be crafted to allow homeowners to remove lawn and replace it with native vegetation; frequently, landscape policies within cities prevent homeowners from converting to native plants. In Eden Prairie, Minnesota, a native plant ordinance was passed that let homeowners remove turfgrass and install native vegetation (www.edenprairie.org; City Code 9.71). Most landscaping ordinances should be reviewed and changed to encourage retrofitting lawns with native plants. Partnering with local native plant nurseries and organizations, such as the North American Native Plant Society (www.nanps.org/), can help communities form coalitions to educate the public and businesses and spread the word about the benefits of using native plants.

To encourage native landscaping in new developments, policies should address various aspects of design, construction, and postconstruction phases. Foremost is the notion of protecting the little pockets of native plants that already occur on each lot. As has been said throughout this book, it is much better to conserve existing native vegetation than to attempt to restore it.

Policies should be crafted that reward developers who retain existing vegetation instead of removing and replacing it. Of course, the successful retention of small areas of natural vegetation is contingent on proper construction techniques and long-term management by homeowners. Thus, policies must address construction and postconstruction issues pertaining to lots. However, few of the current land development regulations address the construction and postconstruction phases of a development. How construction occurs on a site, which long-term management strategies are implemented, and whether people understand the reasoning behind the retention of an existing natural landscape will ultimately determine whether the native patches in yards survive over the long term. Concerning the construction phase, a policy could state that a developer must hire a trained site-construction manager who knows about the natural resource conservation issues that will likely arise during construction, and who is motivated to help the contractors and sub-contractors understand and follow environmental guidelines throughout the construction process. Contractors, too, must be trained and engaged. This will insure that appropriate landscaping techniques are used when installing native plants, natural portions of built lots are properly protected, and invasive exotics are identified and eradicated on a regular basis during construction activities. Concerning the postconstruction phase, a policy should state that an environmental education program must be implemented to guide the care and management of yards and shared landscaped areas throughout the community.

Creating a culture of sustainability within a government is critical in fostering novel solutions that conserve biodiversity. One important step is developing an office of sustainability. This office can educate the planning staff, review development applications, and advise development review boards. Often various departments are involved in issuing a development order, and each must understand and promote native landscaping and construction practices that support biodiversity conservation. Municipalities can lead by example. If a municipality has adopted native landscaping practices in its own operations, it will foster landscaping with natives in the private sector.

Counties and cities can take the lead in adopting environmental practices on urban lots. All county and city properties could follow environmental guidelines that emphasize planting natives, reducing the amount of lawn, and reducing the use of fertilizers, pesticides, and herbicides. Trying out a policy on government property will help ferret out any barriers to, and problems in, following guidelines that the private sector may encounter. Often, interagency conflicts (e.g., between planning and regulatory divisions) become apparent as novel policies are implemented. Such an exercise will help prepare the city and county for the eventual release of the guidelines to the private sector. In addition, a strong regulatory policy can have a dramatic effect on how the private sector maintains landscapes. The city of Quebec passed a law that banned pesticide use on lawns, and this has decreased the use of pesticides in maintaining landscapes (Box 19).

Box 19. The Precautionary Principle and Pesticide Use in Quebec

The city of Quebec passed a pesticides management code that essentially banned the use and sale of certain common pesticides used on lawns in Canada. The policy, which became fully effective in 2006, stemmed from studies on the impact of pesticides on human health, especially in children. While it is debated whether pesticides do cause cancer and other human health issues, and whether they create certain environmental issues, the municipality used the *precautionary principle* as a rationale to ban the pesticides. Essentially the precautionary principle states that, "where there are threats of serious or irreversible damage, the absence of full scientific certainty should not be used as a reason for postponing measures to prevent environmental degradation."

Tracking the impact of the policy, the city found that the ban on the sale of the pesticides was crucial in dramatically reducing the amount of pesticides used; however, the public is still relatively uninformed about alternative practices such as integrated pest management and biocontrol, and additional educational campaigns are needed. Additional resources must be allocated to enforcement and monitoring, something Quebec authorities are trying to address.

Sources: David Susuki Foundation, "Pesticide Free Report," 2008, www.davidsuzuki.org/publications/reports/2008/pesticide-free-oui/; M. Sandborn, D. Cole, K. Kerr, C. Vakil, L.H. Sanin, and K. Bassil, *Pesticide Literature Review* (Toronto: Ontario College of Family Physicians, 2004).

CHAPTER 6

Trails, Sidewalks, and Common Areas

Enjoying the outdoors fosters a connection to and appreciation of local environments, and it promotes community interaction and a sense of community. Building pedestrian trails and sidewalks can help bring people outside to experience nature and interact with each other. Some research indicates that a pedestrian-friendly neighborhood does enhance a sense of community.[1] As expressed earlier, a sense of community is critical to engaging homeowners in adopting environmentally friendly behaviors. If people know their neighbors and are able to communicate with them, then environmental behaviors that are tried by a few people can spread to the rest of the community. In a survey of homeowners in one Florida neighborhood, people reported that they primarily learned about environmental issues and practices from their neighbors.[2] Many biodiversity issues require that whole neighborhoods become involved. For example, if people live around a lake, it takes only a few irresponsible homeowners to compromise the biological integrity of the lake by using too much fertilizer on their property, introducing invasive plants or animals, or irrigating too much. Even strategies to attract wildlife species require a neighborhood to plan for larger patches of habitat, which means that more than one property will have to be involved (see chapter 5). In order to implement neighborhood-wide practices, it is critical that neighbors trust each other and have a rapport.

However, without sidewalks or trails for people to walk on or common areas, such as a children's playground, for people to gather in, opportunity for interactions will be few. Trails provide opportunities for people to walk in their neighborhood and observe wildlife, meet their neighbors, and otherwise connect with their community. A walkable neighborhood offers other benefits as well. Obesity and lack of physical activity are correlated variables, and some studies indicate that walkable neighborhoods could play a role in increasing physical exercise and reducing obesity rates among residents.[3]

WHAT CAN RESIDENTS IN A NEIGHBORHOOD DO?

In neighborhoods that do have private trails and common areas, the maintenance of these systems is usually left up to the residents. Whereas sidewalks next to streets are typically under the purview of local municipalities, private trails and common spaces are usually under the management of homeowners associations. Trails and common areas, if not managed properly, can have unfortunate consequences for biodiversity. When managed properly, trails and common areas can permit people to interact with and enjoy nature without significant impact on local plant and animal communities.

Residents should be informed about the importance of staying on these trails and keeping pets leashed around natural areas (see chapter 3). People or pets walking through significant natural areas can disturb wildlife populations and trample and destroy natural plant communities. While out walking, knowledgeable homeowners should also look for any invasive plants or animals that have gained a foothold. Trails are often conduits for invasive plants, and any invasive exotics should be promptly identified and removed. Plus, all trails require some periodic maintenance, whether they are mulched, cleared, or paved. Frequently trash collects along trails, and periodic cleanups should be arranged to remove litter. It will take resolve and vigilance to keep up with the maintenance of community trails. Perhaps each homeowner could "adopt" a portion of the trail system in a manner similar to the "adopt-a-road" programs, maintaining a section of the trail. In particular, if educational signs about proper trail management were not installed, a neighborhood may want to install such signs. Informed residents will be more apt to use trails properly if they know the ramifications of their actions.

WHAT CAN A DEVELOPER DO?

Often, developers may not be aware of the economic gain of establishing walkable neighborhoods, but such neighborhoods have increased economic value because the properties retail at higher prices.[4] Designing and installing trails, sidewalks, and shared common spaces throughout the community will create the framework for community interaction. This is an important step, because it would be difficult to come into a neighborhood without such features and install them after construction is completed. If space is limited, small neighborhood common areas—such as scattered parks measuring thirty meters square and containing a picnic bench and perhaps some playground facilities—will provide a place for neighbors to gather. Each development project contains site-specific attributes that will dictate the location and quantity of shared open spaces and pedestrian walkways. One should hire a qualified landscape architect who has some experience in the design and management of walkable communities.

Although each site is different, trails, sidewalks, and shared open spaces should have no more than minimal impervious surfaces. To help with stormwater runoff, all trails, sidewalks, and light-traffic paved areas should be permeable where feasible. There are several types of permeable pavements, including porous asphalt or concrete, porous turf, and open-jointed concrete blocks (see chapter 7). Each allows water to soak into the soil, but porous concrete and asphalt require special maintenance—an industrial vacuum must be used on them annually. Neither porous turf nor open-jointed concrete blocks must be vacuumed, unless they are heavily filled with silt, but vegetation growing up between the blocks may occasionally have to be mowed. For trail systems, pavements of any sort may not be necessary, but if the trails go though wetlands, raised boardwalks are preferable because they do not compact or disturb the soil.

One important aspect of a sustainable community is a community garden. Food grown and consumed locally is energy-efficient because it does not have to be shipped far. A local community garden helps residents learn more about food, where it comes from, and how to grow it. In addition to providing locally grown produce, community gardens can help build intergenerational networks and encourage both youth and adults to explore their immediate environment. In a study of several urban community gardens, results indicated that participants developed relationships with local gardeners and learned about soils and plants.[5] Community gardens provide a focal point where people can gather, talk, and reconnect to their environment by growing and caring for vegetables and other plants. Community gardens can provide opportunities for both youth and adults to conduct research, monitor environmental variables within the area, and provide important feedback to residents. To learn more about setting up a community garden, visit the American Community Garden Association at www.communitygarden.org/.

If swimming pools are a desirable feature in a market, building a community pool for the entire community is a better option than an individual pool for each home. This will save a large amount of water and energy. Renewable energy sources can be used to heat the community pool. One option is to install a geothermal heat pump that transfers belowground heat to the pool (see "Geothermal Heat Pumps" at www.energysavers.gov). At depths of two meters or more below the surface, the earth's temperature remains at or near the average annual outdoor air temperature. A geothermal pump's pipes circulate an antifreeze-and-water solution underground, and even during the winter they are warmed by the temperature of the earth. A geothermal heat pump condenses this heat and transfers the heat to the pool.

WHAT CAN A POLICY MAKER DO?

Regulatory or incentive-based polices can encourage the creation of walkable trails, sidewalks, and common areas. One incentive-based option would be to allow developers to build more units on a site in return for including open spaces and trails in the development. Another option would be to fast-track development orders that meet minimal building codes but also have added amenities such as preserved open space and pedestrian-friendly neighborhoods. Where walkable communities are encouraged, policies should require amenities such as educational signs installed along pedestrian routes to inform residents about how their use of such trails could impact biodiversity.

Any incentive-based policy must be carefully researched and monitored for effectiveness. Along with Marisa Romero, one of my graduate students, I investigated the impact of incentive-based policies in several states. We were interested in the uptake of these policies by private developers and builders. Although few policies were considered successful, the most successful ones had these three ingredients: First, government officials and staff explicitly involved stakeholders in crafting the incentive-based policies. Stakeholders were engaged through public meetings and workshops. Information from these gatherings helped to create policies that offered true incentives to the built environment professionals. In some instances where policies did not have a large uptake, government officials had crafted incentives without input from developers. The incentives they offered were not sufficient to attract

developers, so very few took advantage of them. Second, well-crafted marketing campaigns were promoted within the communities and were successful in
educating built environment professionals about the new policies. Where the
uptake was low, the common complaint was that builders and developers simply did not know about the policies. In these cases, most of the effort had gone
into crafting the new policies, and no resources had been allocated for educating the public about them. Good policies merely sat on the books for years.
Third, successful policies required government capacity. Essentially, when a
new construction practice was encouraged, all departments had to understand
this new practice and accept it. In many instances, planners developed policies
to promote new types of construction practices, but the regulatory officials
were unaware of these new practices. Regulatory officials are trained to follow
current regulations, and the new practices may not fit well with what is on the
books. In some cases builders had tried, without support from regulators, to
implement new building practices and had been delayed by outdated regulations. The end result was a delay in the permitting of the construction. This
frustrated builders and cost them more money (in terms of delays) than they
would have spent had they done a conventional development. Governments
must have the cooperation of various departments before implementing a new
incentive-based policy.

    In summary, policy makers should take the following steps to increase
the uptake of incentive-based policies. First, hold a series of public forums
to involve and educate the built environment community. These should be
well-advertised events, and the goal of these forums should be to educate the
public about biodiversity conservation practices, to receive comments, and
to identify both the barriers perceived by the built environment community
and the incentives they would like to see offered. Second, after placing a new
policy on the books, implement a well-funded advertising campaign in print,
on radio, and on local television. In fact, try out the policy on new government properties; this will help work out the kinks in the system and promote
innovative construction techniques for other contractors to see. Third, be sure
that a culture of sustainability is promoted throughout various government
agencies. In particular, identify regulations that may serve as barriers to a
novel environmental construction practice. These conflicts may exist within
any municipality, and I recommend holding internal workshops to determine
potential barriers. If anything, government officials should be flexible, open to
new ideas and different ways of working within current regulations. A series

of reports is available from the University of Florida to help guide governments. These reports evaluate the impact of various incentive-based policies in different counties. Each report contains the actual language of the policies, their success rate, and potential reasons a policy did or did not work well.[6]

However, as stressed throughout this book, one must not forget the long-term maintenance of any design. Policies should reward only the development plans that include solid funding sources for maintenance and explicit management plans for trails, sidewalks, and shared open spaces. One such funding mechanism, a portion of homeowners association dues, can be designated for the upkeep of walkways and open spaces. Biodiversity conservation is enhanced when trails, sidewalks, and common areas are properly maintained.

CHAPTER 7

Irrigation and Stormwater Treatment

Water quantity and quality issues are major concerns for many municipalities. Dealing with water issues usually entails focusing on potable water supply, flooding, and the way local water sources are affected by stormwater runoff. When people consume too much water, this means, of course, that less potable water is available. Flooding can occur when stormwater running off impervious surfaces is not properly managed in urban developments. While improper water management directly affects humans, water consumption and stormwater runoff also affect local natural communities. This is true especially concerning the management of yards. Often when people think about water consumption, they think about water consumed inside the home. In many cases, however, more than 50 percent of the water consumed at home is used to irrigate the yard.[1] Fertilizers and other chemicals used to maintain a yard, especially if they are not applied appropriately, can run off and pollute nearby streams, lakes, and wetlands.

The impact of added nutrients and chemicals on water bodies can be dramatic. Many rivers and lakes do show the effects of nutrient loads from non-point sources such as individual yards. Non-point-source pollution collects from multiple locations, and cumulatively it can have more of an impact than a point source, such as a sewage pipe directly entering a stream. Because non-point sources are caused by a variety of people, such as thousands of homeowners, they are much more difficult to manage. Many states have impaired water bodies as a result of agricultural practices, septic tank leaks, and stormwater runoff; a number of states have implemented best management practices in agriculture and urban areas and have effectively improved the water quality of nearby water bodies (see case studies at www.epa.gov/owow/nps/Success319/index.htm). In some regions of Florida, experts estimate that current pollution in rivers is primarily a result of fertilizers, human waste from septic systems, and animal waste running off nearby yards, neighborhoods, and farms. In one study on Florida's Wekiva River basin, it was estimated that 20 percent of the nitrate load came from residential fertilizer runoff (see the report at www.dep.state.fl.us/water/wekiva/). In particular, reports of algal and toxic algal blooms occurring in Florida's rivers have increased.[2] Algal blooms can deplete oxygen levels in waterways, killing fish and affecting the health of people swimming in these rivers.

The consumption of water, too, adversely affects nearby wetlands and water bodies, because they dry up when there is insufficient groundwater. Rivers around the world now experience reduced flows as a result of climate conditions and human consumption, and some have even begun to dry up.[3] Concern about the supply of potable water has thrown many municipalities into crisis mode, affecting even the right to develop a property in those areas. As a dramatic example, one of Florida's water management districts refused to issue consumptive water permits for new developments in Broward and Miami-Dade counties in 2007, effectively stopping construction of new developments in those counties.[4] Water-well fields were drying up and were barely able to supply potable water to the current population. Water quantity has reached the crisis level in south Florida, and several politicians and community groups have called for building a pipeline to bring water down from northern Florida.[5] This is a controversial subject in the state. The proposed pipeline would be much like the canal system built for Arizona and California, which tapped the Colorado River to provide water to large municipalities like Phoenix and Los Angeles. Such a large diversion of water affects local plant and animal communities, especially those that reside in the waterways being siphoned off.

In subdivisions, stormwater runoff is a significant issue because of the impervious surfaces—buildings, driveways, and pavement—that exist in neighborhoods and prevent rainwater from soaking into the ground. Without adequate stormwater management, surface water can accumulate and flood nearby areas, as well as carry chemicals and excess nutrients to nearby wetlands and other water bodies. During a rain event, the first couple of centimeters of water runoff contain a majority of the human-made compounds that pollute nearby wetlands and waterways. Roads in neighborhoods have oils and other chemicals deposited on the surface, and rain washes away these chemicals; this initial flush of water can enter nearby streams, ponds, and wetlands. In a development, then, runoff must be slowed down and retained to prevent contamination of natural areas and flooding of other properties. In many states, stormwater management systems such as curbs, culverts, and retention ponds are conventionally built in a neighborhood. A civil engineer will calculate soil permeability and the amount of impervious and pervious surfaces, and recommend the quantity and depth of stormwater ponds to be constructed. These ponds serve as a place to retain runoff captured from a storm event. The water evaporates over time, or it percolates into the soil in and around these retention areas.

However, few stormwater management ponds were built for communities before the 1980s; many of the older neighborhoods have only curbs and culverts, so excess water is simply channeled into local streams, wetlands, and lakes. Many people mistakenly believe that water going down into a street culvert flows to the water treatment facility of their local utility, not realizing that anything going down the culvert ends up in local streams.[6] Any nutrients coming off yards, such as grass clippings, fertilizers, and even pet fecal matter, ends up in local waterways. These culverts and channeled conduits are so direct and fast that storm events scour local streams and erode banks. Very little native flora and fauna can survive in such conditions. Urban streams accumulate trash because storm events wash debris into nearby waterways. As a result, once-beautiful urban streams turn into urban blights.

Conventional stormwater systems utilize curbs, gutters, and retention ponds and are primarily designed to retain water on-site and to prevent flooding. While this may make sense from an engineering perspective, often it does not make ecological or environmental sense. In terms of the hydrology of an area, it is not healthy to take most of the water off a site and channel it into one or several locations. Redirecting surface runoff into storage areas minimizes historic infiltration and reduces the contact time water has with soils that could bind and remove pollutants from the water. The best option is to allow water to soak into the soil *where it falls*. Management systems that distribute stormwater are often employed under the guidelines of low-impact development (LID). In LID, stormwater features such as rain gardens and swales are widely distributed across a site and create a treatment train to more effectively remove pollutants from water runoff (Box 20).

LOW-IMPACT DEVELOPMENT

LID is highly compatible with biodiversity conservation because it presents ample opportunity to plant and retain native plants and wildlife habitat. In fact, one of the core principles of LID is to retain as much natural open space as possible. The reasons why LID is both a better method for stormwater treatment and a means for conserving biodiversity include the following.[7]

Groundwater Recharge and Base Flow in Streams

Many stream systems depend on groundwater seepage to maintain base flow between storm events. LID is designed to better match preexisting hydrologic conditions on the site, which means more water is routed back into the soils and less runs off. In urban areas on the coast, conventional stormwater systems

---

Box 20. Stormwater Treatment Train and LID

A stormwater treatment train is a series of components or devices linked together from the top to the bottom of an urban water catchment. It filters the water and lengthens and slows the water's passage through the urban catchment from roof to river, sea, or groundwater. The principle is bioretention and infiltration: biological, chemical, and physical properties of plants and substrates act to filter and improve the quality and quantity of water across a landscape. Low-impact development (LID) is a broad environmental concept, and its primary goal is to create urban developments in a way that minimizes their adverse effects on people and the environment. When LID principles are applied to stormwater treatment, the idea is to mimic predevelopment hydrologic conditions as much as possible. Core principles include controlling runoff at the source and reducing the reliance on centralized downstream treatment strategies. Conventional stormwater treatment systems typically capture water and rapidly move it to storage areas, far from the source of pollutants and the point where rain has fallen.

A variety of treatment trains can be implemented to slow down water runoff and allow treatment close to the source. Essentially, one tries to limit the amount of impervious surfaces and build a series of water-collecting devices that capture water throughout a development. LID features designed to address water quantity and quality issues include swales and filter strips, permeable paved surfaces, rain gardens, and green roofs. A *swale or filter strip* channels the overland flow of

(Continued on page 120)

often convey stormwater to the sea on a large scale instead of allowing it to filter into the ground. And when belowground freshwater is drawn up, saltwater moves inland, killing vegetation and affecting the potable groundwater supply. Keeping the freshwater table up requires water to percolate into the ground inland instead of being directed out to sea.

Soil Fertility

Most LID practices promote conservation of existing natural features and minimizing soil disturbance. In addition to directly promoting biodiversity by retaining whatever plants and animal habitats remain, LID practices keep the topsoil and litter layer intact. If future homeowners want to landscape the area, they will have soils far more conducive to planting than they would have

---

stormwater. It is a shallow, linear depression in the ground that is vegetated and designed to collect and move stormwater runoff. The main function of a swale is to allow the settling and filtering of coarse sediments and contaminants in stormwater, and to transport residual water to other infiltration or detention areas, such as rain gardens or stormwater ponds. *Permeable pavements* allow water to percolate into the ground and reduce the amount of stormwater runoff. *Rain gardens* detain, filter, and evaporate water. They are essentially mini retention ponds that fill up with water after a rainfall. The rain garden is planted in low-lying area composed of specific layers of soil, sand, and mulch to filter stormwater naturally, and it is generally vegetated with a variety of plants. *Green roofs* are vegetated roofs that help to store, retain, and filter water. The structure of these roofs is similar to that of gravel-type roofs, but green roofs have the addition of topsoil and plants. To learn more about green roofs, visit Green Roofs for Healthy Cities, www.greenroofs.org.

All the LID features mentioned here are usually connected, and using LID features can reduce the size of the stormwater ponds needed. Moreover, swales, rain gardens, and green roofs provide opportunities to increase biodiversity across a site. Many different types of native plants can be used in swales, rain gardens, and on green roofs, and these areas also provide habitat for wildlife.

Sources: C. Clark and G. Acomb, *The Florida Field Guide to Low Impact Development: Stormwater Management Practices for Application in Master Planned Community Development* (Gainesville: Program for Resource Efficient Communities, University of Florida, 2008); N. Dunnet and A. Clayden, *Rain Gardens: Managing Water Sustainability in the Garden and Designed Landscape* (Portland, OR: Timber Press, 2007).

if the site had been cleared, soils disturbed, and low-fertility soils added to the site. When soil retains its natural fertility, the homeowner is less likely to fertilize or water the plants.

Soil Fauna

Minimizing disturbance preserves the plants aboveground, and it also maintains a highly diverse and dynamic soil system belowground. Earthworms, nematodes, and small arthropods such as ants and centipedes are conserved. Such soil conservation improves biodiversity by conserving species above and below the ground.

Water Treatment

When spatially distributed infiltration features are used, stormwater comes in contact with a larger total soil surface area than it does in a conventional management system. In addition, having shallower depths in a rain garden or small bioretention areas means there is less head pressure on the water infiltrating the ground, and so the rate of infiltration is slower. Both increased soil surface area and increased contact time are factors that improve removal of unwanted nutrients from the water.

Soil Moisture Mosaic

When multiple stormwater management areas are created throughout a subdivision, the landscape becomes more diverse with respect to soil moisture. This generates an opportunity to increase overall vegetative diversity, because a wider range of microhabitats is available to species.

Natural Stormwater Basins

With LID, stormwater basins can be designed with native vegetation and sculpted to benefit local wildlife. The existence of a more diverse vegetative community in enhanced basins should benefit downstream ecosystems. One of the most dramatic effects of conventional development is a homogenization of the landscape as it fills with turf and a small range of landscaping plant species. This practice limits the recruitment of native species in a watershed. Stormwater ponds often have outlets to other water bodies, so increasing the diversity of the seed source in the stormwater basin could increase diversity downstream and help maintain viable seed stocks in the watershed.

WHAT CAN RESIDENTS IN A NEIGHBORHOOD DO?

If a developer has used LID principles in a neighborhood's stormwater design, it is up to homeowners to maintain these features and look out for problems associated with water drainage. Rain gardens may have been constructed for each property; typically these are low-lying areas where water collects after a rain. They are planted with an assortment of shrubs and other vegetation that thrives in semiwet conditions. Below the surface of a rain garden, the soils are permeable, and a contractor may have installed a layer of gravel and sand to help with water infiltration. The most important thing homeowners can do to maintain rain gardens is to *not fill them in*. These gardens act as mini water retention systems, and if they are filled in with soil, water will not gather at these spots, and stormwater will run off a property, compromising the function of water retention and filtration across a neighborhood. Also, rain gardens must be free of debris, and if a good deal of sediment accumulates, it may have to be scraped off, or the ground may have to be dug up a bit, to retain the water storage capacity of the rain garden. Finally, plants installed in and around the garden may need care just after installation. Occasional watering and inspection of plant health is necessary to help get the plants started.

Swales in fronts of properties must also be maintained, as they are part of the stormwater treatment train. Swales are typically linear depressions situated near roads and are lined with grass or other types of ground cover. The principle of swales is that water is channeled into them after a rain, and as the water runs through these swales, it slows down, increasing soil-to-water contact time. Swales are preferable to cement channels, because water cannot filter through cement. However, if cars or other heavy vehicles are constantly parked on or driven across a swale, the soil can become so compacted that water can no longer soak into the ground, and the soil will become almost like concrete. Thus, homeowners must be diligent and not allow cars or other vehicles to park on or drive across swales. Homeowners also must be aware of debris accumulation within a swale. With too much debris, a dam could form and water could run out of the swale into the street.

If sidewalks and parking areas are made with porous pavement, they must be maintained. There are several types of permeable pavements. One type is porous asphalt or concrete. Underneath the asphalt or concrete surface lies a loose stone layer that serves as a storage area for water before it percolates into the soil. Another type of permeable pavement is porous turf, which has interlocking structural support below the ground to handle foot or light auto traffic. A third type is open-jointed concrete blocks with permeable spaces between the blocks. Essentially, permeable pavement allows water to percolate through the paved areas because the pavement has large holes or a multitude of tiny holes that allow infiltration of water.

Any permeable pavement must be properly managed by local residents, as these areas will become impervious over time if not routinely inspected and cleaned. The most common problem with porous concrete or asphalt is that the tiny holes in the pavement become clogged over time with fine sediment. In fact, several studies have suggested a 75 percent failure rate of porous pavement because of a lack of maintenance.[8] The following recommendations permit successful management of porous concrete or asphalt.[9]

1. Monthly, one should inspect the area to insure that the paved area is clean from debris and sediments. Observe whether the area dewaters between storms. Manufacturers guidelines should be read and followed.

2. Annually, a paved area must be vacuumed (one or more times a year, depending on local conditions) with a special industrial vacuum designed for porous concrete or asphalt.

Swales, rain gardens, and porous pavement are often linked to stormwater ponds. The pond component must be inspected annually to determine if it is functioning properly. Since retention ponds fill with sediment over time, they must be dredged out in order to retain water storage capacity and soil permeability. The creation of a neighborhood stormwater committee can help with the inspection of stormwater management systems.

If the developer has limited the amount of turf in yards to decrease the use of irrigation, residents must resist the temptation to replace landscaped vegetation with lawn. Lawn is typically the largest water hog in a community, and in some localities it is difficult to maintain, often consuming vast amounts of energy in terms of fertilizer applications and mowing. In many instances, lawns have to be replaced because of pest insects or diseases, costing homeowners lots of money. When a property is dominated by turf, its owners may choose to convert the turf areas to landscaped areas or even just stop mowing. When lawn is left unmowed, a diversity of plants will come up, and if designed correctly (with borders, paths, etc.), these "wild areas" can look aesthetically pleasing.

With new landscaped areas or lawns, some type of irrigation system is often necessary. A micro-irrigation or drip system that delivers water directly to the plants is the most efficient, but it must be inspected and adjusted over time. Drip hoses can become clogged and sprout leaks in areas not near the plants. Micro-irrigation tips can break. Research has shown that soil moisture sensors are probably the best products to install in order to water efficiently.[10] Essentially, soil moisture sensors are buried in different areas of a yard and hooked up to a programmable irrigation system. No matter how often the watering system is programmed to come on (say, twice a week), the sensors check to see if the soil actually needs water before they let the system turn on. These sensors save water and increase the longevity of plants, because they do not allow the plants to be overwatered. Overwatering plants can decrease drought resistance and increase disease susceptibility. Underground sensors must be calibrated and cleaned annually to insure proper functioning.

Watering systems that pop out of the ground are typically used for lawns. The calibration and angle of these pop-up heads must be checked so that water is not spraying the road, sidewalk, or house. Misaligned and broken heads can cause significant water loss. One way to check for leaks is to turn off all appliances and irrigation systems that use water, and check the water meter; if the dial is still spinning on the meter, it indicates a leak somewhere in the house or irrigation system. Many homeowners simply use too much water and, because water is still relatively cheap, are not diligent in monitoring use. One need only walk down a street to see sprinkler systems that are watering sidewalks and driveways, and excess water running down the curb. Neighbors can help neighbors by pointing out watering inefficiencies.

If lawns or landscaped areas are watered, the best time to do this is either early in the morning or late in the evening. Watering at the hottest time of the day will result in water evaporating rather than soaking into the soil; watering should not occur between 10 A.M. and 4 P.M. Mulching landscaped areas with three to four inches of mulch will prevent rapid water loss and reduce weeds. Lawns composed of grasses should be mowed at various heights, depending on the type of grass. Bahia and St. Augustine should be mowed at a height of three to four inches, and Kentucky bluegrass and ryegrass around two and a half inches.[11] Mowing grass too short will result in limited root production and thus susceptibility to arid conditions. If the grass is mowed short, it will put most of its energy into growing new leaf blades, and less energy into growing a root system.

Water that falls on the roof of a house can be harvested by using rain barrels or large cisterns. Essentially these barrels or cisterns are positioned under gutter downspouts, and water running off the roof is collected and stored for irrigation during dry periods. Overall, efficient irrigation systems and proper yard maintenance reduce water runoff and consumption, protecting local groundwater. Clean and plentiful groundwater conserves biodiversity, because local wetlands are not affected by excess nutrients and are not in danger of drying up during prolonged droughts.

WHAT CAN A DEVELOPER DO?

For stormwater systems, a developer should utilize low-impact development (LID) techniques that allow rain to soak into the ground where it falls. Some may think that using LID techniques will drive up the costs per lot, but in many cases LID features are actually cheaper than conventional practices (Box 21). The Environmental Protection Agency analyzed seventeen case studies of developments that incorporated LID, and discovered that LID saved money for developers and property owners.[12]

Box 21. Alternative Natural Landscaping Saves on Infrastructure Cost

A more natural yard is not only beneficial for the environment, but it can also save a developer a substantial amount of money. The savings comes from decreased lot clearing and grading costs, less sod needed, and the lower cost of limited irrigation. A subdivision in Gainesville, Florida, called Madera, was designed to maintain natural vegetation in each lot. In a comparison of 2004 costs associated with one of the more natural lots in Madera and a nearby conventional lot, the Madera lot yielded a savings of $1,476 (Glenn Acomb, University of Florida, personal communication, 2010). Most of the savings came from reduced lot clearing, stormwater infrastructure, and turf application (see Table 3). For a subdivision of one hundred lots, the potential savings would be $147,600! Further, a homeowner saves approximately $1,900 annually with a natural yard, because mowing, fertilization, and pesticide applications are not required.

TABLE 3 CAPITAL COSTS COMPARISON OF LID AND CONVENTIONAL
DEVELOPMENT ON A QUARTER-ACRE LOT, GAINESVILLE, FLORIDA
(in 2000–2004 dollars)

Task	LID	Conventional	LID Savings
Clearing/grading	1,612	2,016	+404
Natural area mulch	245	90	−155
Landscape area mulch	665	406	−259
Landscaping	6,485	6,485	–0–
Turf	720	2,331	+1,611
Irrigation	1,275	1,500	+225
Infiltration tank	1,032	–0–	−1,032
Turf reinforcing for parking	845	–0–	−845
Reduced stormwater pond depth	(1,000)		+1,000
Eliminate curb, gutter, and storm drain	(327)		+327
Savings from reduced pavement	(150)		+150
Total	11,402	12,828	1,476

Each site has special considerations, but foremost, one should not gutter, curb, and direct water to only a few retention ponds. It is all about slowing down water runoff and increasing soil-to-water contact time. The use of swales, rain gardens, and building materials such as pervious pavement can help water infiltrate throughout the site. Even the use of green roofs can slow water runoff and help manage stormwater. Trees, shrubs, and other plants intercept vast amounts of water and reduce the strength and volume of rain hitting the ground. Thus, conservation of trees helps with stormwater management. The following steps will help developers design a stormwater system that not only treats water runoff but also improves biodiversity conservation across a site.

Construct Stormwater Basins for Wildlife and Humans

In certain circumstances, stormwater basins (called retention or detention basins) still have to be built. *Retention basins* are characterized by a permanent pool of water that is replenished by incoming stormwater. Discharge takes place through seepage into soil, evaporation, and planned overflow. *Detention basins* serve as excess-water catchments that dry up between storms. The swales around a community are detention basins.

Wildlife habitat can be created in basins, particularly retention ponds, as these attract wading birds foraging for fish and other critters found in the water. The shoreline edges of retention basins should include open areas and areas with native tall and shrubby vegetation. The first few meters of a pond edge is called the *littoral zone* (as an example, see http://edis.ifas.ufl.edu/UW207). A diverse assortment of wading birds will favor ponds with a mixture of tall, short, and floating vegetation occurring in both the shallow and the deeper sections of a littoral zone. To create a littoral zone appropriate for birds, one must not dig the edges of a stormwater pond too deep. A shallow shelf (less than a foot) permits wading birds to forage in the area. Wildlife will only minimally use retention basins that are cut deep (with no shelf at the edge of the pond); are completely surrounded with cement or grass; or have no native vegetation planted around or in the water.

When designed properly, large detention basins can function as playfields or parks for residents. A detention basin that has different levels can shunt the water from most rain events into the deepest areas, and the shallow areas (necessary for very large rain events) can be covered with mowed grass to support leisure activities. Such open space will be a valued amenity in a neighborhood.

Install Efficient Irrigation Systems and Water-Wise Landscaping

Micro-irrigation systems should be installed for landscaped beds, because such systems deliver water directly to the plant.[13] Limiting the amount of lawn solves many water issues, because turf requires a lot of water and care. In southern states, the choice of turfgrass, if used, includes drought resistant varieties, such as centipede, Bahia, and zoysia grass. In northern states, fineleaf fescue varieties can be used; and in midwestern and western states, buffalo grass is a drought-tolerant native grass. For lawn irrigation, soil moisture sensors are a must because they significantly reduce water consumption (Box 22). An alternative to individual watering systems is a central watering system that waters open spaces, yards, and other landscape areas. This takes watering out of the hands of multiple homeowners and lets the watering schedule be determined by a knowledgeable landscaping company. Homeowners association dues would pay for the maintenance of a neighborhood irrigation system. A central system would be the most reliable choice over the long term, since dealing with multiple homeowners can be problematic.

On built lots, reducing the amount of turfgrass and other water-hungry plants will go a long way toward reducing water consumption over the long term. Alternative ground covers, such as perennial peanut (*Arachis glabrata*), can be used for high-traffic areas. The benefit of using these covers is that, once they are established, they require no mowing and only minimal watering. However, such ground covers do not give "instant" landscapes the way turf-grass can, and real estate agents and homebuyers must be educated about the benefits of such landscaping.

As mentioned in chapter 5, the use of fill dirt as a basis for the landscaping should be limited as much as possible. Fill dirt contains little organic matter, so it does not hold water and has few nutrients for plants. Also, fill dirt from

---

Box 22. Irrigation and Soil Moisture Sensors

Several studies indicate that more than 60 percent of the potable water consumed at homes in central Florida goes to irrigation. An examination of irrigation time clocks used by homeowners showed that overwatering still occurred frequently, because most homeowners were not familiar with the appropriate length of time to water different plant materials. Soil moisture sensors offer an opportunity to water vegetation much more efficiently. Typically, soil moisture sensors are hooked up to programmed watering systems, and no matter how the timer is set by the homeowner, the system will not turn on if the sensor has checked the soil and found it sufficiently moist. Thus, these sensors can remove human error from the equation of proper irrigation.

In comparative plots watered by programmed irrigation systems with and without soil moisture sensors, results showed that on average the sensors reduced the amount of water used for irrigation by 60 percent, and turf quality was no different between the plots. The addition of soil moisture sensors to automatic irrigation systems can save a significant amount of water. Soil-moisture sensors sell for anywhere from $75 to $350; in regions where water costs are high, the sensors could pay for themselves in a year or less because of significant water savings.

Sources: M.B. Haley, M.D. Dukes, and G.L. Miller, "Residential irrigation water use in Central Florida," *Journal of Irrigation and Drainage Engineering* 133(5) (2007): 427–434; M.D. Dukes, B. Cardenas-Lailhacar, and G.L. Miller, "Residential irrigation based on soil moisture," *Resource*, a publication of the American Society of Agricultural and Biological Engineers (St. Joseph, MI) (June–July 2005); M.S. McCready, M.D. Dukes, and G.L. Miller, "Water conservation potential of smart irrigation controllers on St. Augustine grass," *Agriculture Water Management* 96(11) (2009): 1623–1632.

elsewhere, or even borrowed dirt (e.g., from dug out stormwater retention areas), can contain high levels of undesirable nutrients such as phosphorus, which will leach out over time. Thus, alternative methods should be used to meet the engineering requirements of homesites. As mentioned earlier, homes can be built on stem walls to meet the minimum flood requirement for an area, so raising the level of the lot will not be required. Removing the topsoil may be necessary in some cases: while this destroys soil biota, such as earthworms and small insects, the removed top soil can be stored on-site and used as fill dirt at a later date. This removed topsoil will lack healthy soil biota, but it will contain more organic matter then sterile fill dirt does. The best solution is to identify portions of lots that can be left alone, and allowed to retain the soil horizon and plant structure.

Limit Where Construction Vehicles Can Go

As mentioned in chapter 3, more than 90 percent of the relative compaction of the topsoil occurs within the first three passes of a heavy vehicle. Thus, heavy earthwork machines should follow a specific route in and out of a site. Heavy machinery should not be allowed to run about the site, because compacting the soil will reduce water infiltration and ultimately increase water runoff that can affect nearby conserved areas and surrounding habitat. In a study on soil compaction on a construction site, construction activity reduced infiltration rates by 70 to 99 percent.[14] It did not matter how heavy the vehicle was. The infiltration rate was so low in some areas of the construction site that the seemingly pervious soils had infiltration rates similar to those of impervious surfaces. Keeping the soil free of heavy compaction will reduce stormwater runoff during construction and in future years.

All contractors, site managers, and subcontractors should be trained in appropriate earthwork-machine operation. The message in any such training session should be that soil compaction destroys the ability of an engineered stormwater treatment train to properly store water. If designated areas that will eventually become swales, mini retention areas, and rain gardens become highly compacted, their ability to store water will be greatly reduced. In addition, strict covenants can be developed, including fines for noncompliance and rewards for compliance. Training and covenants will help to engage people during the construction phase and help to insure the long-term functionality of a stormwater treatment train designed to store water and remove pollutants close to the source.

Create an Education Program That Highlights Stormwater Treatment and Irrigation

The long-term management of stormwater and irrigation systems depends on homeowners understanding the purpose and function of such systems. It is critical that homebuyers are educated about, and understand the purpose and upkeep of, rain gardens, swales, micro-irrigation, and so on. I strongly suggest the installation of an education system with signs, a Web site, and a brochure that contains information about the purpose and management of a neighborhood stormwater system and irrigation systems in yards (see chapter 4).

WHAT CAN A POLICY MAKER DO?

Because curb, gutter, and retention pond systems have been on regulatory books for decades, many barriers become apparent once a developer tries to implement low-impact development techniques. Regulatory barriers must be removed, and incentives established, to encourage new types of stormwater management practices. Built environment professionals have been reluctant to try new practices for fear of retribution from regulatory agencies that may not understand the techniques or be supportive. However, this is changing as regulatory agencies adopt LID practices. As a first step, municipalities can develop their own LID projects as a demonstration of the way developments could be designed and to engage residents in local water quantity and quality issues (Box 23). LID projects on government property and retrofits of neighborhoods will help work out any kinks between planning and regulatory departments and simultaneously establish model sites for built environment professionals to view. Eventually, policies calling for curbs and gutters can be replaced with policies calling for low-impact development.

As mentioned throughout this book, special attention is warranted for policies that address issues during construction. Construction activities can compact the soil to a point where even pervious surfaces have infiltration rates that are similar to those of impervious surfaces. Moreover, silt fences that are not functioning can compromise nearby wetlands and water bodies that have been conserved. Regulatory procedures must be adjusted to help insure that construction activities follow specific guidelines that minimize soil compaction and stormwater runoff. Perhaps stiffer fines must be levied when silt fences are not maintained or when construction vehicles enter zones that are off-limits. More oversight is likely warranted to monitor construction activities, which means hiring additional inspectors to observe how contractors are behaving across a construction site. But while fines and oversight have their place, teaching contractors about why certain rules are in place can go a long way to enhance compliance. All contractors should take a course on low-impact development. This course should cover the concept of stormwater treatment trains and explain how compacting the soils compromises the ability of multiple water-retention features to store water. Such courses on LID may promote a sustainable culture within the contractor community, and contractors may become much more diligent about designing and managing construction sites in ways that minimize impacts on the environment.

Regarding LID practices, the one note of caution brought up by municipalities is that the success of practices such as swales and rain gardens is contingent on whether homeowners manage these sites appropriately. Regulators are

---

Box 23. Seattle's Street Edge Alternatives Project

Seattle embarked on a project to retrofit a street with a naturalized drainage system and street-designed approach. The overall goal of the Street Edge Alternatives Project was to slow the water down and allow natural bioretention areas, located alongside a neighborhood road (Second Avenue NW), to capture water runoff from the street. The redesign of the street has several notable features. First, the road was narrowed, creating less impervious area and more space for plants and soil to absorb rainwater. Water is directed to planted swales located along both sides of the street. These swales allow water to filter into the soil, where soil particles and plants capture water pollutants (Figure 21). Second, vegetation in these swales includes mostly native Pacific Northwest grasses, shrubs, and trees, which serves an important function, capturing water runoff and increasing local biodiversity. Third, because the street is now narrow and curved a bit, vehicle speeds have decreased and people feel safer walking along this road. Fourth, the neighbors have been involved from the beginning, and because they are engaged, the street edges have been well-maintained by the neighborhood.

To measure how much water is captured, Seattle Public Utilities and the University of Washington conducted a monitoring study. Monitoring stations were placed downstream of the project, and during the project's first three years, data showed that 98 percent of wet-season and 100 percent of dry-season stormwater runoff has been eliminated into nearby Pipers Creek.

(Continued on page 132)

cautious because the treatment train for stormwater is located on individual lots instead of a centralized system. The LID features may not function properly if homeowners do not maintain these features properly. To help mitigate this, each developer should be required to demonstrate a long-term management strategy, such as an education program to engage homeowners. Developers may state that this is an extra burden, but policy makers could create incentives such as permit breaks to help pay for such educational systems. If a homeowners association or homeowners do not appropriately manage the rain gardens and swales, a municipality can create a new policy that levies fines or other punitive measures to get a neighborhood to comply. This is important, because many agencies will be uncomfortable adopting new low-impact practices if no contingency plan is in place for potential failures in long-term management.

Figure 21. Bioretention swales planted with native plants along a residential street, Seattle, Washington. Photo by Drena Donofrio.

Source: Adapted from Seattle Public Utilities, *Street Edge Alternatives*, n.d., www.seattle .gov/util/About_SPU/Drainage_&_Sewer_System/GreenStormwaterInfrastructure/Natural DrainageProjects/StreetEdgeAlternatives/, accessed 2010.

Concerning irrigation practices, policies (either regulatory or incentive based) should be created to limit the amount of turf used throughout a site. A number of different municipalities are offering incentives or have passed regulations to promote efficient irrigation practices (Box 24). Examples include the East Bay Municipal Utility District, California (www.ebmud.com); Colorado Springs Utilities, Colorado (www.csu.org); and Bernalillo County, New Mexico (www.bernco.gov). Limiting turf automatically solves many of the water quality and quantity issues within a community. Where turf is permitted, policy should address irrigation systems. In particular, the requirement of soil moisture sensors can save a municipality a good deal of water, because the sensors reduce by 60 percent the amount of water used for irrigation (see Box 22). Also, policy should encourage the use of drought-resistant grass species, native plants, and perhaps alternative ground covers that require less maintenance. One promising ground cover to replace lawn in warmer climates is perennial peanut (*Arachis glabrata*). This remarkable subtropical plant requires little maintenance, because it is resistant to drought, nematodes, and pathogens and requires minimal fertilization. It produces an attractive yellow flower, is reported to be comfortable to walk on, and requires no mowing.[15]

When any new irrigation practice is instituted, municipalities have to be sure that the contractors are knowledgeable about proper installation. In east Pasco County, Florida, the developer of a subdivision called Lake Jovita used a variance on a landscaping and irrigation ordinance (Box 24), which involved soil moisture sensors. The development's first phase was approved before the ordinance was passed, and the developer did not have to comply with the new code; but other phases were not exempt. The developer argued that because the development had previously been approved, the entire development should be exempt. A compromise was made in which the developer could exceed the 50 percent non-drought-tolerant plant rule. This essentially allowed the developer to install more turfgrass. The Development Review Committee approved a code variance, based on three criteria: (1) in all future building on the entire development, the developer would be required to use soil moisture sensors; (2) amendments to the deed restrictions would require the installation of soil moisture sensors in turfgrass and landscaped areas of newly built homes; and (3) the developer would provide homeowners with educational materials about the use of the sensors.

However, follow-up on installation of the sensors showed that they had not been installed properly. Apparently, the hired contractor did not think soil

Box 24. Landscaping and Irrigation Ordinance, Pasco County, Florida

The following policy was implemented on February 26, 2002, in Pasco County, Florida (2005 population 429,065, per the U.S. Census Bureau).

Purpose

To reduce water consumption by providing minimum standards for the development, installation, maintenance, and preservation of water-efficient landscaping and irrigation systems in residential lots. This ordinance is mandatory for all single or multifamily residential developments or commercial developments.

Summary

The ordinance applies to single-family or two-family residential lots with irrigation systems and Class I, II, and III developments (i.e., small, medium, and large commercial areas). The county requires the contractor to submit the completed certification of compliance, showing that all irrigation and landscape components have been incorporated. Irrigation contractors fill out a self-certification application, and the final inspection is conducted by a county-approved, certified inspector. After the final inspection, the county issues a certificate of compliance.

Key provisions of the ordinance: (1) a maximum of 50 percent of the plant materials used can be non-drought-tolerant, (2) turfgrass with excellent drought tolerance may exceed the 50 percent rule, (3) a minimum of 30 percent of the plant material, other than trees and turfgrass, must be native, (4) turfgrass must be in irrigation zones separate from other landscape irrigation zones, (5) narrow landscaped beds (four feet wide or less) must not be irrigated unless micro-irrigated, and turfgrass areas must not be less than four feet wide, (6) sprinkler spacing must not exceed 55 percent of the sprinkler's diameter of coverage, (7) sprays and rotors must have matching application rates within separate zones, (8) sprinklers must not spray water onto paved areas, (9) a functioning rain shutoff device must be utilized in automatic irrigation systems, (10) organic mulch must be at least three inches thick, (11) a maximum of 50 percent of the on-site green space must be allowed to utilize irrigation techniques other than micro-irrigation, and (12) where available, reclaimed water must be utilized for irrigation.

The ordinance originated in the Southwest Florida Water Management District, which encouraged local governments to consider adopting water-efficient landscaping ordinances. The Native Plant Society in the county also encouraged the insertion of language specifying that the use of native plants was required. Model landscape ordinances from other counties were used as a base to develop the language for this ordinance.

Current Impact

The limited number of inspectors has made it difficult to inspect all new landscape-irrigation systems in developments for which contractors have sought certification. More inspectors and randomized inspections of developments could help increase compliance with the ordinance. An estimated 57 percent of new homes in Pasco County have irrigation systems, and compliance with the ordinance could provide significant water reductions.

An evaluation of the ordinance by Tampa Bay Water revealed the parts of the ordinance with which builders complied, and those with which they did not comply. Generally the sites evaluated met the requirements concerning sprinkler spacing, spray overlap, separate zones for rotors and sprays, and no rotors or sprays irrigating areas less than four feet wide. However, several sites did not comply with certain other requirements. These included requirements to create separate irrigation zones for turfgrass and tree or shrub beds; to prevent application of water to impervious areas; to use micro-irrigation in plant beds; to limit the percentage of irrigated area in turfgrass; to plant at least 30 percent of the area with native plants; and to use micro-irrigation for at least 50 percent of the irrigated area.

Pros and Cons

The ordinance was not accepted enthusiastically, and several residential and commercial developers and even residents have used innovative techniques in order to avoid compliance. Some developers have planted drought-resistant grass such as Bahia grass in areas of yards without irrigation. After the homes were sold, the owners removed the Bahia grass and planted St. Augustine grass and extended the irrigation systems. Initially, the building and landscape industry did not provide much input concerning the ordinance. In order to provide additional opportunities for them to voice their concerns, public meetings with builders and landscape architects were held, and their input is now being used to make amendments to the ordinance. For example, according to the previous ordinance, the irrigation contractor filled out self-certification papers. A new amendment now requires certification to be completed by somebody approved by the county administrator. This will put more pressure on the builders to ensure compliance with the ordinance.

The ordinance can be found at www.pascocountyfl.net/devser/sd/dr/ldc/l603 .pdf.

Source: Adapted from M. Romero and M.E. Hostetler, *Policies That Address Sustainable Landscaping Practices*, EDIS circ. 1519 (Gainesville: Wildlife Ecology and Conservation Department, Florida Cooperative Extension Service, Institute of Food and Agricultural Sciences, University of Florida, 2007). Available at http://edis.ifas.ufl.edu/UW253.

moisture sensors worked, and had not hooked them up to the irrigation system (Chris Dewey, University of Florida Extension agent, personal communication, 2003). The problem was found only because a county extension agent monitored the installation. The developer hired another contractor, who was informed about the performance of these sensors and proper installation. *The take-home message here is that monitoring is critical,* and that every new ordinance should be tracked to find out whether it is having the intended impact.

CHAPTER 8

Wildlife-Friendly Transportation Systems

Whether moving within their home ranges or migrating from one region to another, wildlife species traverse a landscape. Subdivisions have roads that could inhibit the movement and dispersal of wildlife species. Because of the danger of crossing roads, many species may not attempt to cross them, and cars kill many individuals that do. Roads have the potential to disconnect wildlife populations and effectively stop animals from getting to and from certain natural areas. As mentioned in chapter 3, connectivity is important for wildlife populations, because the health of a regional population of animals is contingent on the ability of individuals to get from one area to the next. Isolated populations are prone to extinction. Even animals moving between habitats within their home ranges are exposed to the dangers of automobiles.

Wildlife species—especially mammals, reptiles, and amphibians—are highly susceptible to speeding vehicles. Moreover, when large animals such as deer cross a road, they pose a danger to drivers. Cars can kill birds, as well, whether raptors feeding on roadkill, or other types of birds that walk across roads or fly across at car height. Residents in a neighborhood, developers, and policy makers all play a role in minimizing the number of roadkills in subdivisions. It is important to consider strategies to make the automobile transportation system in subdivisions friendlier to wildlife.

FIGURE 22. Wildlife box culvert under a four-lane road that passes through Paynes Prairie Preserve State Park, Florida. This wildlife passage is used by reptiles, amphibians, and mammals. Photo by Dan Pennington, 1000 Friends of Florida.

WHAT CAN RESIDENTS IN A NEIGHBORHOOD DO?

The fewer cars on the road, the less chance an animal will be hit. Biking, walking, and using mass transportation are ways to get to a destination without using a car. Carpooling is another way to reduce the number of vehicles on the road and is also a good way for neighbors to interact. If a neighborhood or city has good walking and biking paths, people can bike to the nearest bus or train station. In many cases, people are too busy to map out alternative transportation routes, and sharing information is one way to engage neighbors in using other transportation options. The creation of an alternative transportation club can keep neighbors informed about latest events and opportunities. Alternative transportation information could be distributed through a neighborhood newsletter or Web site. Organizing events such as a "Bike to Work Day" is a good way to raise awareness. If a neighborhood is not friendly to bikes, neighborhood modifications can be discussed at a homeowners association meeting. Typical modifications include installing speed humps, decreasing the speed limits on neighborhood roads, and installing bike racks at various venues. When enough voices ask for them, funds to install bike and walking lanes throughout a section of town could be provided by local government.

If underground wildlife passageways are installed to accommodate wildlife moving from one natural area to the next (Figure 22), then these passageways must be monitored and managed when problems arise. Trash and other debris can clog road culverts, making them difficult for species to use. Road culverts designed to accommodate wildlife have a layer of natural substrate inside for the animals to walk on, and this substrate may erode away over time. More substrate must be installed when this happens, because many species do not like walking on artificial surfaces such as corrugated iron. Where walls have been placed to prevent animals from climbing up onto the road, vegetation must be managed, because over time the vegetation will creep over the walls and animals will climb it and attempt to cross the road, bypassing the below-ground culvert. In summary, any installed wildlife passage must be managed over the long term, and it is up to the residents near these wildlife passages to be vigilant and help maintain them.

WHAT CAN A DEVELOPER DO?

A subdivision can be attractive to homebuyers if the road system is attractive and promotes safe use for pedestrians, bicycles, and wildlife. Traffic volume and accidents are major concerns for people living in neighborhoods. The noise and air pollution of streets with heavy traffic can prevent neighbors from talking or gathering on sidewalks near these streets. Many people desire community amenities along roads, such as shade, sidewalks, street lamps, benches, and other features that promote the health and safety of drivers and local residents. The following guidelines offer some design and management strategies that developers can implement to create safe and healthy neighborhoods, by slowing traffic down and minimizing collisions between wildlife and vehicles.[1]

- Install narrower streets with on-street parking; this reduces vehicle speeds. The recommended width for streets is between sixteen and eighteen feet, with parking on one side (a road of this width is called a lane), or between twenty-two and twenty-six feet, with parking on two sides (called a street). Lanes and streets are typically short and run from two to six blocks. Main roads that connect town centers or different neighborhoods are called avenues. These contain a median (twelve to sixteen feet wide), and the paved roads on either side of the median are twenty-four feet wide with on-street parking, and seventeen feet wide without. Avenues can extend up to one mile. Fire and ambulance services are able to use such roads and their widths comfortably. Vegetative swales alongside roads can separate pedestrians and vehicles, and these swales provide a place for native plants, wildlife habitat, and stormwater treatment.

• To reduce the amount of pavement needed, longer blocks may be preferred. Because long blocks encourage higher traffic speeds, speed bumps and curves should be installed on the longer streets.

• Design the lots with minimal front yards, installing front porches close to the sidewalks and garages in the back with alleys for access. Having porches and small front yards makes a neighborhood more inviting for pedestrians and interactions among neighbors. Street trees should be planted next to on-street parking. Use native trees, because they are adapted to local conditions, meaning they require less maintenance, and can serve as wildlife habitat. Planting strips should be a minimum of six feet wide, with five-foot sidewalks on both sides. Such features give the feeling of a more enclosed space, and this reduces traffic speed while at the same time encouraging pedestrian use of sidewalks.

• To further slow traffic, install neck downs (roads that are narrow near intersections), curved streets, and narrow intersections with tight turning radii (a corner radius of about fifteen feet).

• Traffic speed limits should be fifteen to twenty miles per hour.

Lighting along streets should also be considered when creating a wildlife-friendly transportation system. Streetlights can negatively influence wildlife in a number of ways. Depending on the species and location, light pollution can affect both resident and migrating animals.[2] Light pollution threatens wildlife by disrupting biological rhythms and otherwise interfering with the behavior of nocturnal animals. Residential areas near beaches that have nesting sea turtles should have cutoff illumination, because light pollution endangers baby sea turtles. Sea turtles lay eggs on beaches, and when they hatch, baby sea turtles find the ocean because it is usually the lightest area at night (it reflects moon- and starlight). However, artificial lights located behind beaches lure recently hatched sea turtles away, and they become disoriented, wandering across roads or along beaches until a car or predator kills them. Artificial lights also alter amphibian foraging and calling behaviors, because some salamanders do not like to forage in bright light, and certain tree frogs do not call in bright conditions. Artificial lighting seems to be taking its largest toll on bird populations. Nocturnal birds use the moon and stars for navigation during their biannual migrations, and lights are an artificial attractor. Birds often crash into brilliantly lit broadcast towers or buildings, or circle them until they drop from exhaustion. Lights affect even wildlife corridors, as some animals tend to avoid corridors exposed to artificial light.

Developers should meet Dark Sky standards for their subdivisions (Box 25). For lighting along roads, choose wildlife-friendly lights, which are shielded from the sky and pool their light on the ground. Shielding lights helps prevent artificial light from inundating any conserved natural areas. But while cutoff lights direct their light toward the ground, they still create some horizontal light pollution that can affect wildlife populations. And so, near

---

Box 25. Harmony's Dark Sky Project

The developers of Harmony made an executive decision to make the community dark-sky friendly (see www.darksky.org/). Essentially the goal of a dark-sky community is to reduce light pollution stemming from artificial light. Dark sky standards utilize full cutoff illumination that shields lightbulbs so that light is not emitted toward the night sky or surrounding natural areas. In a full cutoff light fixture, the lightbulb does not extend below a lampshade. The benefits from such lighting are many: it allows people to view the stars, and it helps limit the impact on wildlife populations, because less light infiltrates nearby natural areas where wildlife resides.

Figure 23. A full cutoff streetlight in Harmony, Florida. Photo by J. W. Vann.

(Continued on page 142)

natural areas, developers should reduce the number of outside lights installed, lower the heights of outside lights, and decrease the intensity of lights. Using light-colored surfaces in areas that require lighting could reduce the amount of light needed. Lights should not be installed near wildlife passages, such as culverts under roads, because some species avoid well-lit areas.

For most subdivisions, roads are a necessity, and some roads may bisect natural areas; portions of these roads may warrant some type of wildlife crossing. It is not always possible to reroute roads to accommodate the movement of wildlife species. The following is a discussion of wildlife passageways for both terrestrial and aquatic species.

Roads and terrestrial animal movement. The first step is for the developer team to identify which animal species in the area may need wildlife-friendly road crossings; this will vary depending on location and surrounding habitat. One should hire a local wildlife biologist to identify such wildlife species and to locate areas where wildlife will most likely cross a road. Once a location is identified, several options are available. First, one could install several speed bumps to reduce traffic speeds, and install wildlife crossing signs. This will make drivers aware of an area where animals are likely to cross. In many cases, some kind of underground crossing may be desired. Often, natural wildlife crossings coincide with streams and other riparian areas; thus a culvert that must be located under a road anyway could be designed to accommodate animals. Some important considerations for culverts:

The developers of Harmony made a conscious decision to limit light pollution wherever possible. They installed low-intensity outside lights, and along streets and walking areas they placed full cutoff illumination (Figure 23). Residential lighting too is shielded. Outdoor fixtures are fully shielded or are recessed into porch ceilings to provide a soft welcoming glow at night. Alleys at the rear of houses are not lit; instead, garage lights on individual homes provide lighting as needed. The results have been dramatic, as people can see the stars in the neighborhood. In fact, people have remarked that they are amazed the pathways are so well lit and yet they can look up and see the stars. Harmony is used to educate people about astronomy. Harmony even has an annual Dark Sky Festival that draws thousands of people to the community to gaze at the stars.

Sources: Adapted from G. Golgowski, "Harmony Is a Dark Sky Community," 2009, www.wec .ufl.edu/extension/gc/harmony/darksky.htm.

- Be sure that some dry areas occur within the culvert even during extremely wet conditions. If the culvert is completely filled with water, terrestrial animals will not use it.

- For small animals such as salamanders, install a one-foot-diameter pipe next to the larger culvert to allow the safe passage of smaller critters that may not like to use large, box culverts.

- Use a natural substrate along the bottom of any culvert, as animals are reluctant to walk on steel or other unfamiliar materials.

- Install speed bumps above these culverts, as not all animals will use the culvert and may go across the road. Also, do not install lighting in these areas, because light prevents wildlife from using a culvert. Plant vegetation screens around the culverts that do not block the entrance to the culvert but provide shelter and cover for animals.

- In some cases, fencing may be required to funnel wildlife into the culverts. A road bisecting a wetland is likely to be raised several feet; the sides could be vertical cement walls, which will prevent animals from climbing onto the road and force them to go through the culverts. Any vegetation growing over the sides of such roads must be cut back so that it does not allow critters to climb up onto the road.

- Some species avoid culverts with dark, tunnel-like interiors, which occur especially in very long culverts. Install skylight grates on top of the road, which allows light to enter midway into the tunnel.

A more detailed discussion about appropriate wildlife crossings can be found in these two references: "High, Wide, and Handsome: Designing More Effective Wildlife and Fish Crossings for Roads and Highways" and "Planning for Transportation Facilities and Wildlife."[3]

Once wildlife road crossings and corridors are identified, homes along these passageways must be given special design and management considerations. First, some kind of buffer must be established between the wildlife corridor and backyards. Backyards cannot simply end at the edges of a significant wildlife corridor, because noise, lights, and pets will disturb wildlife movement patterns. A ten-to-thirty-meter buffer should be situated between the yard and the corridor. No fences should be allowed within a buffer or corridor, to allow the free movement of animals. In particular, humans and pets should be strictly forbidden to walk within a designated wildlife corridor, because this would disturb wildlife. People purchasing homes in these areas should be educated about the importance of wildlife corridors and should help maintain them; they must watch for neighbors and pets that may intrude into these wildlife corridors. With an engaged community, wildlife corridors and passages across roads have a better chance of being used by wildlife.

Roads and Aquatic Animal Movement

If roads cut off connections between portions of water bodies such as wetlands or streams, this restricts the ability of fish and other aquatic species to disperse from one area of the water body to another. The first step is to identify which aquatic species in the area may need culverts; this will vary depending on location and surrounding habitat. One should hire a local aquatic biologist to identify such animal species and to locate areas where aquatic organisms may cross under a road. Roads that cross wet areas such as streams will require culverts for drainage purposes, but to make culverts usable by aquatic organisms the culverts must be designed in a certain way. The following are some important considerations:

- For the movement of most native freshwater fish, wetlands and other water bodies must be connected by streams at least ten centimeters deep, depending on the species of fish. Note that long stretches of fast-flowing or polluted water, flap gates, and overhanging culverts all act as impassable barriers. To permit effective fish movement, the bottom of the culvert should be below grade, and rocks or other materials should be added to slow water flow.

- Sited culverts should follow the original direction of the stream. Making right angles to the natural course of a stream (to go through a culvert) will decrease the chance of successful fish passage, as there is more turbulence at such entrances. A no-slope design is also preferred to reduce velocity inside the culvert.

- Natural substrates should be added to culvert bottoms to aid the movement of critters besides fish, such as frogs, turtles, crayfish, and snails.

- Shorter culverts are better than long ones, especially where the water velocity is high. Some species of fish may not be able to swim the entire length of a long culvert with rapidly flowing water.

WHAT CAN A POLICY MAKER DO?

Developing policies to encourage developers to implement transportation systems that promote biodiversity should be a priority for policy makers. Every city will have slightly different issues and somewhat different solutions to promote safe vehicular traffic and movement of wildlife. To improve wildlife movement, it is important to identify corridors that could serve as passages for wildlife. Once critical areas are identified, workshops and public forums must be held to identify strategies to insure that these wildlife linkages are either restored or conserved. Only by identifying these wildlife linkages well in advance of development can meaningful solutions be derived. As mentioned throughout this book, it is better to conserve first than to restore—restoration of critical wildlife linkages takes much more effort than initial efforts to set aside land before it is developed.

Creating wildlife-friendly transportation systems in subdivisions may cost a little extra money, since building underground passages or rerouting roads will incur an additional cost, requiring support from the developer. Sometimes, best practices to make roads safer for wildlife may cause misunderstandings between city departments, such as a fire department's reluctance to use narrowed roads in neighborhoods. All such issues must be addressed from the very beginning, before a policy is implemented, to limit the amount of controversy and the number of hoops a developer must jump through. Switching from a vehicle-dominated transportation system to a more pedestrian-friendly and wildlife-friendly system with options for greenways takes coordination among all the government departments that regulate growth.

To reduce vehicular traffic, policy makers can encourage developers to build structures that support alternative transportation systems, such as bus stops and parking areas for bikes. By offering incentive-based policies, cities can insure that subdivisions will contain features that encourage residents to use alternate means of transportation. On properties that have wildlife-crossing issues, incentives should be devised for the developers who go the extra step to insure that wildlife can cross their property safely. This may entail rewards—such as permit breaks or housing density bonuses—for planned developments that reroute roads or engineer culverts that accommodate wildlife needs.

CHAPTER 9

Environmental Covenants, Conditions, and Restrictions

In the United States, covenants, conditions, and restrictions (CC&Rs) are legal documents (sometimes called deed restrictions) that dictate how properties in a subdivision look and how they are managed. CC&Rs, which derive from English common law, are procedures for property ownership and land transactions. Simply stated, CC&Rs are promises that the buyer makes as a condition of purchasing the land from either a developer or a previous owner. The CC&Rs are filed with the land records in the county or city where the land is located. When developers subdivide a piece of land, they cut an existing piece of land into two or more pieces, called parcels, lots, or units. Having created a subdivision, developers usually place restrictions on how the lots may be used by later homeowners. Of course, the idea behind CC&Rs is to help insure that lots within a master-planned community have a look and feel that is consistent with the intent of the developer and with what people thought they were buying. The CC&Rs run with the land, so that even if the land changes owners, the CC&Rs are still operational.

Often during build-out of the community, the developer enforces these CC&Rs, but upon completion of the community the regulatory function is turned over to a homeowners association (HOA). Any homeowner can sue any other homeowner who does not abide by the CC&Rs. In reality though, much of the enforcement is in the hands of the HOA board. Once CC&Rs are placed on a property, they are difficult to change. CC&Rs usually contain provisions that permit amendment by majority vote or, in some cases, a specified supermajority. However, the law in Florida and some other states has imposed an important limitation for amending CC&Rs. If the amendment affects the lots nonuniformly, the proposed amendment must be approved by all the lot owners, even if the CC&Rs themselves say that they can be amended by a majority vote. It is often believed that zoning overrules CC&Rs. For instance, if a property is rezoned for commercial purposes, people may think that it could be used for commercial purposes regardless of CC&Rs limiting the lot's use to a single family home. This is a misconception. CC&Rs and zoning ordinances are completely independent of one another.

Much of the language of CC&Rs addresses aesthetics and the maintenance of property, such as how yards look and how they are maintained. In a study of CC&Rs in Phoenix, Arizona, many of the landscape clauses addressed aesthetics (e.g., instructing homeowners to keep shrubs trimmed) but many of the

---

Box 26. CC&Rs in Phoenix, Arizona

Covenants, conditions, and restrictions, and how homeowners associations (HOA) enforce the CC&Rs, can influence the look of residential landscapes. In a study of residential landscapes in Phoenix, researchers compared the yards of homes in neighborhoods with and without CC&Rs. They found that those with CC&Rs had less turf coverage than neighborhoods without CC&Rs. Over 60 percent of the front yards in neighborhoods with CC&Rs had a desert design and lacked turf. Also, more residents in neighborhoods with CC&Rs identified their landscapes as "desert," as opposed to "oasis" or "mesic," types of landscapes that have more turf. However, only 33 percent of homeowners in neighborhoods with CC&Rs preferred desert landscaping. Thus, what actually is in the yards of some of them runs somewhat counter to homeowner preferences. These findings suggest that CC&Rs and HOAs had successfully promoted desertlike yards even though residents prefer landscapes with turf. CC&Rs may set the tone for a neighborhood, and landscaping practices may follow whatever is spelled out in the document.

In a separate study in Phoenix, researchers explored the landscaping language of CC&R documents that are registered with various neighborhoods. They wanted to determine which landscaping features were governed by HOAs through CC&R documents. In their textual analysis, researchers inspected landscaping language for three management categories: vegetation and pest management, water

(Continued on page 148)

documents addressed species composition and even whether turf was prohibited or required (Box 26). Because there are restrictions placed on properties, CC&Rs can either promote or hinder biodiversity conservation in a neighborhood. For example, if the language of CC&Rs specifies that each front yard within a neighborhood must contain at least 80 percent turf, then it would be difficult for a homeowner to replace the turf with native plants, especially if there is an active HOA. CC&Rs should contain language that promotes biodiversity conservation in a neighborhood. The following are ways in which residents, developers, and policy makers can make CC&Rs more conducive to biodiversity conservation.

---

management, and species composition. The species composition category had such things as rules prohibiting or requiring turf, and the types of plant species that were prohibited or required. Of the thirty-five CC&R documents analyzed, 37 percent either required or prohibited certain plant species. Concerning lawns, 20 percent of CC&Rs either required (14 percent) or prohibited (6 percent) turf. One document stated that a maximum of 50 percent of turfgrass was allowed in a yard. The study also mentioned that many of the CC&Rs did have plant lists but did not offer a rationale for why certain plants were encouraged and others prohibited. This study shows that CC&Rs can contain specific language that could shape how yards are designed and managed. Because HOAs actively regulate the composition and maintenance of neighborhood yards, the language of CC&Rs is a powerful social construct that can affect biodiversity conservation throughout neighborhoods.

In summary, to help conserve biodiversity within individual yards, CC&Rs must contain not only specific clauses that prohibit or allow certain plant species or landscaping practices but also information about why these clauses are in the document. This way, homeowners and associated HOAs can understand why certain species and management practices are prohibited (or encouraged) and how individual actions can aid in the conservation of local plants and animals.

Sources: C.A. Martin, K.A. Peterson, and L.B. Stabler, "Residential landscaping in Phoenix, Arizona, U.S.: Practices and preferences relative to covenants, codes, and restrictions," *Journal of Arboriculture* 29(1) (2003): 9–17; K.L. Larson and S.J. Hall, *Social-Ecological Dynamics of Residential Landscapes: Human Drivers of Management Practices and Ecological Structure in an Urban Ecosystem Context* (Tempe: Arizona State University, Global Institute of Sustainability, 2008).

WHAT CAN RESIDENTS IN A NEIGHBORHOOD DO?

Often, older CC&Rs have outdated regulations, and the document should be reviewed and updated to reflect current practices that would promote biodiversity. This usually requires a community discussion and a neighborhood vote. Neighborhood block parties or potluck dinners can be used as a forum in which homeowners can discuss the topic of biodiversity and natural resource conservation in the neighborhood. The goal for updating CC&R documents would be to allow practices that could improve biodiversity in yards and throughout the neighborhood. Allowing the removal of turf, preventing the use of invasive plants, and permitting backyards to revert to natural habitat are a few of the practices that could benefit native plants and animals.

In many cases, it may be too difficult to legally change a CC&R document. Alternatively, a neighborhood discussion could lead to the election of a HOA board that supports biodiversity conservation measures. Then, individuals could petition for a variance to implement practices that are prohibited by the current CC&R document. The HOA board would then allow variances that enhance biodiversity conservation on individual properties.

WHAT CAN A DEVELOPER DO?

A CC&R should explicitly state environmental and biodiversity practices related to the homes, yards, and neighborhoods. At a minimum, the CC&R must allow homeowners to convert their lawns to native landscaping. The document can address a mixture of regulated, prohibited, and encouraged activities. The CC&R should encourage homeowners to experiment with their yards to promote biodiversity. The document should outline and provide reference documents, preferably ones that can be accessed online, about how to provide wildlife habitat, along with a list of native plants that do well in the area. A list of native plants will help homeowners to select the most appropriate plants for their yards. Simply stating that homeowners must use native plants will be too ambiguous. Information on the dangers of feeding wildlife, particularly mammals, should be included. Feeding of problematic animals such as bears, deer, raccoons, alligators, and possums should be strictly prohibited. The danger is that these animals will lose their natural fear of humans and become aggressive, tear up property, and in the worst case scenario, attack humans.

Part of the document should address the use of pesticides, herbicides, and poison baits. Pesticides are usually nonspecific and will kill not only the pest insects but also beneficial insects in the area, such as bumblebees and other pollinators. Many herbicides, if not applied properly, have the secondary effect of killing nearby vegetation and affecting aquatic life, such as fish. Integrated pest management practices should be encouraged or required as a way to manage pests. Biological controls, such as ladybugs to eat aphids, and benign sprays, like soap sprays, should be encouraged as a first step. The document should also refer homeowners to reference documents about illegal chemicals that should not be used, and about proper application of allowed chemical sprays when environmentally friendly means have been tried and have failed. In particular, fertilization of lawns and landscape plants should be reduced as much as possible to minimize nutrient runoff into nearby water bodies. If fertilizer is necessary, the use of slow-release organic fertilizers should be encouraged. Reference documents would contain educational material for homeowners about proper fertilization rates and procedures.

Important prohibitory language that should be included in a CC&R concerns invasive plants and animals. Residents should understand which plants are considered invasive, and be prohibited from planting them. Cats and dogs off leash can have significant impacts on wildlife, and the CC&R should have strict leash laws. Even the release of smaller pets such as exotic toads, snakes, fish, and lizards can have dramatic consequences for local wildlife and should be prohibited.

If natural areas are part of the community, guidelines in the CC&R should address the behavior of people who live near these significant areas. Driving motorized vehicles through the conserved areas, walking off marked trails into conserved habitat, dumping trash and yard debris, and using white floodlights are just a few activities that can disrupt wildlife populations and affect plant communities. Prohibited activities should be listed, and appropriate behaviors should be encouraged. To see a working example of a CC&R document that addresses a few of the environmental concerns I've described here, refer to the CC&R drawn up by the town of Harmony (http://edis.ifas.ufl.edu/UW248).

WHAT CAN A POLICY MAKER DO?

The best action that policy makers can take is to create policies that encourage developers to write CC&Rs that explicitly address biodiversity issues for a subdivision. Often biodiversity conservation is left out of these documents, but a discussion of it helps communities to understand it and adopt landscaping practices that benefit local plants and animals. In particular, crafting a model CC&R would help local developers address environmental and conservation issues pertinent to a given area. Each city has particular concerns for certain wildlife and plant species, and any model CC&R language should be adapted to reflect local conditions.

CC&Rs can also address LID features on individual properties, such as rain gardens and swales designed to collect and store water as part of the neighborhood stormwater treatment system. As discussed in chapter 7, regulatory agencies such as state and county departments of environmental protection are wary of allowing designed water-retention features to be maintained by homeowners. CC&Rs can help alleviate some of these concerns by explicitly addressing the maintenance of LID features on individual properties. This would at least give the HOA some authority to correct homeowner behaviors that compromise the functionality of such features as rain gardens and swales. An LID section of a CC&R document should contain information about proper maintenance and include details about the purpose of LID features on each individual property. Policy makers could request that such language be inserted in CC&Rs for master-planned subdivisions.

CHAPTER 10

Certifying Green Communities

With heightened international and national awareness about sustainability, both the public and governments are putting pressure on businesses to offer more environmentally friendly choices for consumers. There is a growing market for master-planned communities containing green features such as energy-efficient homes and natural open space. Independent certifying groups have evolved to produce green standards for developers so they can receive awards or certificates that establish their communities as green. Developers can then market these communities to consumers and get premium prices for their homes.

The validity of green certification programs has been questioned, because many of these programs can be gamed to achieve green certification. Certification programs are in their infancy, and for the most part their effects, particularly concerning biodiversity conservation, are marginal. I am not saying that these organizations and their staffs are not dedicated; they truly want to create green communities, and most of these organizations have very good educational information and trained staffs to help developers and communities. Certifications do serve as an important role—they help start a conversation about a different way of building a community. It is just that, in practice, having a menu of green standards and a point system opens up the practice of achieving minimal standards. The process becomes more about public relations than about significantly reducing the environmental and ecological impact of a community. The following is a summary of some of the problems with green certification standards.

A typical certification program has a menu of points that a developer or community must address to achieve a certain level of sustainability. The problem is that each site and building is different, and having a standard menu of options does not yield the best design and management strategy for minimizing impact on a given site. It is virtually impossible to have an inclusive menu of options that provides the maximum environmental benefit for a given site, because each site offers a unique set of constraints and opportunities. Thus, a developer could choose the easiest design or easiest management practices and still gain the most points—but this would not necessarily lead to the best environmental practices for a site. Examples of this are many. The U.S. Green Building Council's LEED (Leadership in Energy and Environmental Design) point system has been criticized.[1] The council is the premier certification organization in the United States, and it has done a lot of good; before it came into existence in 2000, no standards for building design existed, and any development company could call itself green. The LEED program has created a buzz for green building construction.

Problems with the LEED rating system indicate problems in other programs, so I use it here as an example. The following are a few issues associated with the LEED certification program.

- The cost for just the paperwork and hired consultants to get a building certified can be high. Even for small buildings, the costs can exceed $25,000.[2] Such money may be better spent to update a building or improve existing landscaping.

- The point system for buildings gives equal credit to certain practices. This may not lead to the best design for reaching one's goals, given local conditions, but it is the easiest. In Boulder, Colorado, for example, a recreation center received a point for installing an electric vehicle recharging station, but only six electric vehicles existed in Boulder at the time, and the charging station was used less than once a year.[3]

- Many innovative solutions are not on the checklist, even though they would save significantly on energy or some other environmental factor.

- The program's bureaucracy tends to focus on meeting the standards, instead of on collaborating with developers to find unique solutions.

- Most certifying programs emphasize design and do not offer many credits for construction and postconstruction management practices, such as engaging residents or installing a long-term management program. As made clear in this book, management is an essential aspect of biodiversity conservation, and any design can be compromised over the long term if construction and postconstruction issues are not addressed.

- In the LEED certification program, a developer can achieve green status for a subdivision by implementing certain green practices while ignoring others. To illustrate this point, a development may be certified because of its energy-efficient homes, even though the developer has done practically nothing to address environmental landscaping, to engage residents, or to preserve wildlife habitat. It may be that the site has critically endangered wildlife species in or around the development, and that more effort should have been dedicated to conserving it.

Most of the green certification programs include only a few points for conserving and restoring biodiversity. Many of the programs concentrate on energy, livability, and transportation. As I've noted in this book, connections exist between energy, livability, transportation, and biodiversity. For example, trees can decrease energy consumption by shading buildings, and if one were to plant native trees, this could promote biodiversity as well. It would take only a bit of tweaking to include more points for biodiversity in the certification programs' checklists. In general, specific actions and language relating to biodiversity have been left out of the equation and must be addressed more thoroughly.

Several states have launched certification programs centered on wildlife conservation. Wildlife-friendly communities tend to emphasize wildlife and wildlife habitat conservation, and focusing on this incorporates many of the biodiversity conservation practices and strategies discussed in this book. Wildlife certification programs concentrate on the conservation and management of natural areas, on the incorporation of native plants into landscaping, and on management practices that focus on minimizing impacts on surrounding environments. A particularly good example can be found in the Wildlife Friendly Development Certification Program that was launched in North Carolina in 2010 (Box 27). This certification program is remarkable because it allocates points to the design, construction, and postconstruction phases; this is not done in most other certification programs. Another relatively new certification program of note is the Sustainable Sites Initiative (www.sustainablesites.org). It addresses ecological and social issues during design, construction, and post-construction phases. The North Carolina Wildlife Friendly Development Certification Program and the Sustainable Sites Initiative contain probably the best guidelines and point systems for conserving biodiversity in subdivision development. I highly recommend exploring these programs.

Granted, many certification programs are new and the process is evolving; thus, change may be around the corner. Even the LEED program has gone through several iterations updating the program. Most certifying groups have very good guidelines and educational materials to help built environment professionals build a green community. The certification process is simply a bit dysfunctional in some instances. Since a developer using a green certification

---

Box 27. Wildlife Friendly Development Certification, North Carolina

The voluntary Wildlife Friendly Development Certification program is a result of a collaboration between the North Carolina Wildlife Resources Commission, the North Carolina Wildlife Federation, and the North Carolina chapter of the American Society of Landscape Architects. This program recognizes developers who truly incorporate natural resource protection into their residential developments (www.ncwildlife.org/WFD/index.htm). The program has a detailed certification handbook that explains the best design and management practices to implement with regard to wildlife habitat conservation. Associated with the handbook is a spreadsheet with criteria; points are allocated for various designs and management practices. Some of the criteria are required, some are optional for extra credit, and the rest are a menu of options that developers can implement to obtain enough points to get certified.

Because each building site offers a suite of opportunities and constraints, a developer interested in pursuing certification works with a review team consisting of North Carolina Wildlife Resources Commission biologists and North Carolina Wildlife Federation members. After the developer fills out a predesign checklist, he or she submits this to the review team so they can become familiar with the site. The review team then consults with the developer to help him or her identify opportunities to conserve wildlife habitat on the site and to minimize impacts on the surrounding environment. Recommendations that come from this meeting are meant to help the developer make decisions most appropriate for the site.

(Continued on page 156)

group has access to its educational materials, this should help with the design of a green community—a good first step. However, let me stress again that most green certification programs emphasize design and *not management issues during the construction and postconstruction phases*. Without correct construction techniques and long-term management, even the best design is doomed to failure.

WHAT CAN RESIDENTS IN A NEIGHBORHOOD DO?

Homebuyers should *never* take green marketing or a green certificate at face value. One must do some investigation. In particular, every homebuyer should ask the real estate agent or developer questions about design and management practices that pertain to biodiversity. A developer concerned about the functionality of the subdivision will have addressed management issues during the construction and postconstruction phases. For example, homebuyers should ask whether the conditions, codes, and restrictions address environmental and biodiversity issues. Next, the homebuyer must evaluate the strengths and weaknesses of the subdivision. It may be that a buyer values watching wildlife

---

Next, the development receives a score based on criteria specified in two sections. In section 1, titled "Development Conservation Design," a developer obtains points for a design that maintains a conservation emphasis while addressing the placement of roads, conserved areas, and buildings. Here, much of the emphasis is on preserving natural areas and, in particular, priority habitats that have been identified by the North Carolina Wildlife Action Plan. As outlined in section 2, titled "Development Construction and Post Construction," the developer acquires points according to how construction activities are managed, and from educational materials and nature-based activities that are created for the residents. To obtain certification, an applicant must earn at least half of the potential points available in each section, and together these must amount to at least 55 percent of the total potential points. Once certified, the development is annually recertified to insure that homeowners maintain the community as it was when originally certified. A development called The Woodlands at Davidson (www.thewoodlandsat davidson.com/), located in Davidson, North Carolina, has enrolled in the certification program and is being used as a pilot case to test the certification process (see Box 28).

from home, and so conserving wildlife and biodiversity throughout the neighborhood is a priority. A subdivision may be good at conserving energy as a result of building design, but it may not conserve biodiversity—for example, the developer may not have used native plants on lots, and the open space may be covered primarily by turfgrass. Consequently, one should investigate various sustainability issues and determine how green a community is according to what one values.

If the developer has answers, one should investigate further and see if other members of the development team—real estate agents, builders, and contractors—have a similar vision. Their answers will say much about how successfully the original intent for the community has been implemented. Also, questioning local government officials and policy makers about the reputation of the developer can reveal how trustworthy a developer is and whether the community could be another example of greenwashing.

One can rate a development's level of sustainability based on several aspects, such as biodiversity, energy, water, livability, and so on. When evaluating the biodiversity category, the recommendations in this book will help one to formulate questions and develop ratings. When looking at the ways a developer has addressed design, construction, and postconstruction issues, I would ask the following questions.

1. Was setting aside significant native trees and natural habitat a priority within the development? If so, are management plans and funds available to help manage these trees and areas over the long term?

2. Are native plants a major part of the landscaping palette for both private spaces and shared open spaces?

3. Is keeping the amount of turfgrass and impervious surfaces to a minimum a goal for the community?

4. Have stormwater treatment trains been built according to LID principles?

5. Do construction guidelines for individual lots address topsoil and natural vegetation conservation?

6. Have significant wildlife corridors been identified and conserved?

7. Did the developer hire an environmental consulting firm and contractors who are knowledgeable about and supportive of biodiversity conservation?

8. Are education programs and activities available to help engage residents in biodiversity conservation?

When buying a home, it behooves a homeowner to understand and become familiar with all the green design and management features of a community. Often a range of management issues is associated with each green feature, and it is up to the residents to act as watchdogs and be caretakers of homes, yards, and neighborhoods. Some certifiers, such as Audubon International, require the developer or subdivision to reapply each year to retain green status. One should become involved with and knowledgeable about the recertification process and certifying group; these groups, once problems are identified, can help provide solutions. Feedback, both positive and negative, to the certifying agency can help improve their green program, as any certification must evolve over time. One should not stop there but should also speak with policy makers, built environment professionals, and other homeowners about challenges and solutions in a neighborhood. Any feedback will help raise the bar on constructing green communities and help improve the environmental movement across the country.

WHAT CAN A DEVELOPER DO?

At the very least, investigate green certification groups and programs, because they offer valuable lessons and ideas on ways to build a green community. Several government and academic programs, such as the Department of Energy's Building America program (www.doe.gov) and University of Florida's Program for Resource Efficient Communities (www.buildgreen.ufl.edu), may not offer certifications but do contain a good deal of information and consulting advice on ways to create resource-efficient and healthy communities. When attempting to attain certification with any program, one should resist the temptation to go for minimal standards. It is more important to adopt practices that most benefit the site. Each site has its own set of environmental issues and solutions that may not be adequately addressed by a certifying program. Instead of adjusting plans to make the most points, which may not make the most environmental sense, one should speak with the certifying agency and see if there is some flexibility. If not, or if the program is too cumbersome, document what was done and use this in marketing materials. Architects and developers were constructing green homes and communities before certification, and their projects are probably just as green as certified projects.

When collaborating with a certifying group or participating in a green building program, one should provide feedback, both positive and negative, to the group, as this will help improve green building programs and create successful communities. In particular, notice whether points are given for construction and postconstruction methods and strategies. As seen within this book, these are critical development phases that typically are not addressed. Within professional societies and circles of friends, one should discuss the pros and cons of different green designs and management features and even, if warranted, put in a few good words about collaborating with a particular certification group or green building program. Word of mouth among built environment professionals carries a lot of weight when certification groups and green building programs are attempting to become mainstream.

The sales office and sales staff should be trained and well aware of the green features and vision of the community. Nothing looks worse to a potential buyer than a salesperson who is unaware of the green features. Interested homebuyers will probably ask (if they have read this book!) sales personnel about the green design and management practices implemented during the design, construction, and postconstruction phases. A knowledgeable staff can really sell the green features in a neighborhood. If a subdivision is certified, the sales staff should be aware of the certification program and be able to state its pros and cons and where the development exceeds or fails to meet the program's standards. Offering a required environmental education course(s) will help raise the awareness of the sales staff and, in turn, help educate the general public about biodiversity and natural resource conservation.

Model homes or sales centers are used to show potential homebuyers what the community is like. At these locations, the building and landscaping must showcase biodiversity conservation practices such as the use of native plants and the minimization of turfgrass. Often, this is the first experience of biodiversity conservation that a homebuyer will have, and it should be genuine. The sales center should provide educational materials about green features, which should contain information about and options for going above the green standards offered in the community. Landscaping choices, above some basic level, could be offered, with options ranging from 100 percent native plants to a mixture of native and ornamentals. If the benefits of natives are marketed, more homebuyers may go for this option, making the community even greener. Arranging several environmental packages that go beyond the standard one will give people the option to explore the idea of having more environmentally conscious homes and yards.

WHAT CAN A POLICY MAKER DO?

Policies can make third-party certifications a requirement, but policy makers must be careful when selecting the certifying agency and determining how points are allocated for certification. As mentioned previously, many point-based certifications are problematic and may not produce green communities that are much different from conventional communities. In particular, a certification program may heavily emphasize energy and water conservation, and award very few points for biodiversity conservation measures. Green development certification is usually achieved by obtaining points in various sustainability categories, and a developer could attain certification by incorporating green features found in only one or two categories. For example, certification could be achieved through incorporating green features in the energy and transportation categories, and very few features in the biodiversity and water categories. In this scenario, a developer would obtain a third-party certification with little or no thought about biodiversity conservation. If a government utilizes a third-party certification program, policy makers must evaluate whether the program has enough *mandatory* points in the biodiversity category. The certification program should not only look at design, but it should also require strategies to address construction and postconstruction issues. A good example is the North Carolina Wildlife Friendly Development Certification (see Box 27).

Certification programs attempt to increase the adoption of new practices and reward people who do so. Most of the principles and practices discussed and recommended in this book would apply to a certification program that has biodiversity conservation as its primary goal. However, developers and other built environment professionals must be educated about the different strategies to use during design, construction, and postconstruction. To conserve biodiversity, governments should develop or collect a number of reference documents that contain guidelines, and even detailed resource manuals that demonstrate such things as the identification and conservation of natural areas, construction techniques that have minimal impact on conserved trees and natural areas, the installation of low-impact stormwater treatment trains, and how to develop an environmental education programs for residents. Ultimately, local green subdivisions could serve as model neighborhoods that provide developers with a firsthand look at green practices. As mentioned previously, showing working models of this sort can go a long way toward increasing the uptake of alternative design and management practices. Without resource manuals or working examples, most people will likely balk at adopting alternative practices, because they will be apprehensive about figuring out a new way of doing things.

If financial incentives such as the reduction of permit fees are offered to developers to promote green building practices, and certification fails, then the developers should return the money. In the case of construction issues such as violations during construction that are not rectified, the building permit should be revoked and construction halted. For postconstruction issues in cases where density bonuses have already been rewarded, punitive measures, such as increased impact fees, should be applied if a developer does not follow through and fails to address long-term issues.

In the end, policy makers may have to create their own certification program or adopt a known certification program and create points that address biodiversity, construction, and postconstruction issues. It may take a bit of extra money, but municipalities could hire a trained planner who is aware of the pros and cons of green development and of certification standards as they relate to biodiversity. Such an individual can help a municipality work out the best strategy for encouraging the construction of developments that conserve biodiversity. One could also train existing staff on the ins and outs of green building designs and practices as they pertain to biodiversity. Most municipalities have building inspectors, and they must inspect buildings and issue permits for occupancy. Through a series of trainings, these building inspectors could be provided with the knowledge to reward extra points for builders who adopt green construction practices that conserve biodiversity.

The ability of municipalities and third-party certifiers to monitor what happens during the construction and postconstruction phases is a tricky issue. Government regulators rarely visit a site multiple times during the construction phase and again years after build-out. To address this, government agencies could hire a few inspectors trained in inspecting and evaluating biodiversity conservation practices as they are implemented during construction and maintained over the long term. To fund a group of inspectors who can monitor construction and postconstruction phases, governments will have to be creative. For instance, if a developer is creating a green development and is going through the process of getting a construction permit, then perhaps the city or county can award a reduced permit fee or a density bonus, and in exchange the developer can fund independent inspectors who visit the site during construction and postconstruction. These visits would generate a report to help the developer correct problems and monitor the environmental effects of certain building and landscaping practices, such as maintenance of the silt fences during the construction phase. If enough developers take advantage of this type of policy, and some taxpayer money can be allocated, then perhaps an office of green inspectors could be established to help monitor the construction process and evaluate the effectiveness of practices that address biodiversity conservation. Another option is a special tax initiative approved by the public; special tax initiatives have been successful in establishing a pool of money to buy critical land within counties, and the same strategy could be used to promote green development programs.

Certification programs are one tool that can be used by governments to help direct the way future and current neighborhoods adopt biodiversity conservation practices. In general, policies and government programs create the enabling conditions under which built environment professionals and citizens can adopt new practices that appreciably improve biodiversity conservation within cities. However, no certification program is perfect, and it will take some evaluation to determine the benefits of a given program. *I cannot state strongly enough the importance of monitoring, because one can learn much from monitoring programs.* Such feedback can be used to further modify and improve certification initiatives that attempt to raise the bar of sustainability.

In Summary

We could go over the cliff. You would hope not. You would hope that people see what needs to be done. It's not rocket science. It's not difficult. It's not even all that costly. It's actually about the way you think about the world.

—Tim Flannery, Australian ecologist

Throughout this book, I have emphasized the importance of design and management, the three phases of development (design, construction, and postconstruction), and the hierarchy of decisions made in and for green communities (by residents, developers, and policy makers). To conserve biodiversity, a variety of people must be engaged in the creation and maintenance of a subdivision development. Policy makers create the enabling conditions in which developers and residents implement novel solutions; developers build the framework of a community, which shapes how homes, yards, and neighborhoods perform; and residents make daily decisions that promote or hinder the conservation value of subdivisions. Subdivision design, while important, is not enough, and construction and postconstruction management must become points of emphasis in green developments. Without this holistic treatment, green developments will become dysfunctional communities that originally had good intentions.

Although it will be a big leap to overcome the inertia, history, and politics that have shaped conventional developments across the country, I see things changing. Environmental, political, social, and economic factors are intersecting in new ways to help maintain a balance between humans and nature. World opinion about the environment, from global climate change to local environmental issues, has shifted—from how to circumvent these issues to doing something about them. We must concentrate now on urban communities and realize that what goes on in every home, yard, and neighborhood has both local and global implications. Synergies are occurring across historically opposed groups, such as conservatives and liberals, and environmentalists and businesspeople. These synergies stem from win-win scenarios that include such things as a country achieving oil independence and energy conservation; people living in healthy, active communities that have natural areas; the public buying green; and green industries reaching their tremendous growth potential. The recent economic downturn in the United States and around the world has created a unique opportunity to forge new paths. It is no longer business as usual, and economic opportunities are there for the taking by forward-thinking individuals.

If we think of green communities as existing along a continuum from one (doing nothing) to ten (doing everything), most green communities will lie somewhere in the middle. There will be no perfect situation, as each site has unique opportunities and constraints stemming not only from the actual landscape itself but also from local societal values, policies, and market forces. It will truly take innovative leaders—whether they are residents, developers, or policy makers—to shift conventional thinking. But each piece of the puzzle must be addressed in order to create *functional* green subdivisions: residents, developers, and policy makers must understand, accept, and become engaged in the whole process of creating and maintaining communities that notably conserve and restore biodiversity.

This book is a primer to help policy makers, developers, and residents build and manage subdivision developments that conserve and restore biodiversity. It is based on the idea of not only advocating particular actions but also providing the rationale and ecological understanding behind the action. The following checklists summarize essential tasks that should be undertaken when constructing a development or subdivision. In many cases, it will not be practicable to implement all these measures, but each one that is adopted will enhance the survival of native species and enhance the human experience and comprehension of nature in a neighborhood. The checklists highlight strategies pertaining to residents, developers, and policy makers, and each encompasses a variety of actions that have been detailed in the book.

Residents

- Understand and help teach neighbors about proper management of conserved natural areas and trees, yards, trails, and common areas.
- Create a conservation club to help maintain or restore natural areas.

- Understand how to properly maintain the irrigation system and low-impact stormwater treatment train, such as rain gardens, swales, and permeable pavements.
- Support and encourage the use of native plants in landscaping and the reduction of turfgrass.
- Be aware of wildlife corridors, and keep them free of elevated lights, noise, and human or pet activity.
- Keep pets away from all natural areas, and do not feed problematic wildlife species.
- Review covenants, conditions, and restrictions, and help the local homeowners association to incorporate clauses that address biodiversity conservation.
- Investigate the development's green community certification to see how it addresses biodiversity conservation.
- Support local politicians and government staff who promote the creation and maintenance of green developments.

Developers

- Conduct natural resource inventories of the site and surrounding lands in order to identify and conserve the most significant natural areas and trees.
- Cluster the built areas to conserve large natural patches, with less edge, that connect to nearby natural areas both within and outside the site.
- During construction, minimize soil disturbance and compaction by minimizing routes for heavy machinery, properly fencing trees and marking natural areas, and designating storage areas for building materials.
- Use stem wall construction for buildings on individual lots; this conserves soils and minimizes grading and the use of fill dirt.
- Develop strict construction covenants, and train contractors in sustainable construction practices, such as proper silt fence installation and maintenance.
- Use landscape designs and construction strategies that will minimize future wildlife-human conflicts.

- Install a low-impact stormwater treatment train throughout the neighborhood.

- Require native landscaping to be used on all lots and common areas, and minimize the use of mowed turfgrass.

- Create landscaping guidelines that emphasize native landscaping, minimize soil compaction and use of fill dirt, and preserve existing vegetation.

- Limit roadways and provide ways for animals to cross under or over the roads.

- Implement an environmental education program that highlights the role of residents in maintaining conserved natural areas and the biodiversity in yards.

- Create a management plan for natural areas and a funding source to support best management practices.

- Have covenants, conditions, and restrictions that inform residents about biodiversity conservation and that regulate how homeowners manage their yards.

Policy Makers

- Develop policies that encourage or require compact developments and the conservation of significant natural areas and wildlife corridors.

- Require that landscaped areas contain native plants, and that developers minimize the amount of turfgrass in both shared and private lots.

- Encourage or require developers to have a management plan for natural areas in their developments, as well as funds to support good conservation practices.

- Develop policies that encourage or require low-impact stormwater treatment trains and efficient irrigation.

- Develop guidelines for construction activities so that builders protect natural areas, large trees, and topsoil.

- Create a culture of sustainability among government agencies to help staff search for and accept green construction practices.

- Offer continuing education courses to engage the private sector and teach them about construction practices that conserve biodiversity.

- Require or encourage developers to implement an environmental education program to engage residents.

- Provide resource manuals and case studies about biodiversity conservation in order to educate and engage the private sector.

- Require developers to have covenants, conditions, and restrictions that address biodiversity conservation.

- If using a green certification program, determine whether the program awards enough points for biodiversity conservation.

- For any policy that addresses biodiversity conservation, monitor the impacts of the policy and look for ways to improve it.

- Create a countywide biodiversity conservation strategy that specifically includes design and management criteria for subdivision development.

Do not underestimate the importance of having one or two model yards, subdivisions, and cities. These working models help pave the way for the next iteration of green. As an example, my colleagues and I have had some success and failure with a local green community called Madera, in Gainesville, Florida, a project on which we consulted through the University of Florida's Program for Resource Efficient Communities. Madera has proven to be useful as a demonstration project, and we have invited real estate agents, developers, landscape architects, scientists, and students into the community and shown them the various green features. In particular, Madera demonstrates that native landscaping can work. Real estate agents and developers were skeptical about the reduction of turf, use of native plants, preservation of snags, and use of porous pavement. Most believed that this type of landscaping would not sell in today's market. Only when we took developers and real estate agents through the subdivision did they change their minds. We showed them that the lots sold quickly, had reduced infrastructure costs, and actually sold for more per square foot than conventional homes nearby. The economic bottom line is a powerful motivator; but increasingly, green developments must demonstrate how alternative development practices can increase the bottom line and improve local environmental measures, enhance livability, and create outdoor spaces that conserve our natural heritage.

In any city, it will take some effort to get initial projects off the ground, because the challenges and solutions involve a variety of stakeholders. Every phase of a new development requires due diligence and determination to see a project through to fruition. Of primary importance are the motivation of the developer and how receptive the city or county planning staff is to the implementation of designs and management strategies that maximize biodiversity conservation. Every subdivision development is different, having its own opportunities and challenges. Not only is each parcel of land unique, but also local political, economic, and cultural forces play an important role in shaping how subdivisions are created and maintained.

It is highly unlikely that all the design and management practices discussed in this book will be adopted for any given project. Some may be relevant for one site but not another, and in some cases local regulations and market conditions may make it easy to adopt one practice but not another. However, having a vision to build a conservation subdivision automatically places a development on a specific path, and this first step helps to overcome barriers, either perceived or real. To help people see how a subdivision development designed to conserve biodiversity could be created in the real world, I selected a development in the town of Davidson, North Carolina, as a final case study (Box 28). In my discussion of it, I present the path this development took and the interplay of policy makers, developers, and the public. This case study highlights the principles and practices mentioned in this book, and it demonstrates that if all stakeholders share the same vision, a variety of biodiversity conservation practices *can* be adopted in a planned subdivision.

Honest monitoring, evaluation, and communication of the successes and failures of green developments are needed. The one advantage we have in today's society, which we did not have in the past, is improved, global communication. The Internet age and mass media connect people from all over the world; information can be quickly conveyed to almost anyone. Societies can learn from the successes and failures of projects attempted in a variety of environments and cultures. Most of the ideas in this book are not complex or expensive; they simply require a shift from conventional development practices to a methodology that explicitly respects our connection to the land and our vanishing natural resources. I hope this book will spark innovation in all sectors of society, and that our collective thoughts will push the green agenda, continually improving on old ideas and coming up with new ones.

Box 28. The Woodlands at Davidson, North Carolina

The developers of The Woodlands at Davidson (www.thewoodlandsatdavidson. com/) followed a unique path to create a wildlife-friendly subdivision. The visionary developers worked with local policies, a forward-thinking town-planning firm, and input from several conservation groups, which resulted in a development that incorporated a variety of design and management practices to conserve biodiversity. It is instructive to look at this process from the design phase to the postconstruction phase.

Design: The sixty-six-acre site was zoned as a rural planning area. Local policy required that developers set aside 50 percent of open space, and that they prioritize preserving mature hardwood forests, wetlands, and contiguous tracts of open space. This enabled them to set aside significant natural areas. The developers, Greathorn Properties and Ridgeline Development Corporation, hired a town-planning firm, the Lawrence Group, which embraced the idea of a more natural neighborhood, to design the layout of the site. The goal was to let the land speak first and to situate the roads and built lots in a way that maximized wildlife habitat. With input from town staff, the developers, local biologists, and the North Carolina Wildlife Federation, the designers found a way to conserve about 38 percent of the property as open space in this fifty-six-home subdivision (Figure 24). The developers received bonus credit for facilitating public access to the open space and building roads with narrow rights-of-way, and this credit reduced the open space requirement to 38 percent. Through the middle runs a wildlife corridor positioned alongside a riparian area with significant stands of hardwood forest on either side. Several lot lines, roads, and the main entrance were moved to save legacy trees and to provide more contiguous wetlands and avoid creating isolated patches. Trails were established in the open space for residents to enjoy nature. The overall design established a framework in which to conserve biodiversity.

Construction: The construction site manager understood the wildlife-friendly goal of the subdivision and worked to minimize soil disturbance and impacts on conserved areas and significant trees. One of the first steps he took was to designate the limits of clearing for the contractor by walking the site with him and pointing out markers where earthwork machines could go. Grading was strictly limited to roadways, and parking areas for heavy machinery were in designated areas. Silt fences were properly maintained, and orange, tree-safe fencing was positioned at the drip lines of marked trees and natural areas. Instead of curbs and gutters,

(Continued on page 170)

Figure 24. Master site plan for The Woodlands at Davidson, where 30 percent of the area is composed of conserved hardwood forests and wetlands and another 8 percent is made up of a planted orchard and a common green area with planted wildflowers. Courtesy of the Lawrence Group.

swales were built along the streets to capture stormwater runoff. Fewer sidewalks were constructed, because of the natural trail system, which minimized impervious surfaces. One interesting conflict happened during road construction. State regulations required the construction of temporary sediment basins, which typically would be sited in low areas along the roads, and the construction of these basins would have meant that many trees would have to be cleared. Working with local officials, the developers were able to move the locations of some of the required basins to future homesites. This compromise both met state regulations and minimized the clearing of trees. Furthermore, the road culverts were somewhat wildlife-friendly at the stream crossing, because they were built with the bottoms below grade to allow a more natural surface substrate.

In landscaped sections of both common areas and private lots, native landscaping was required. Before planting the common areas, the developers consulted with the North Carolina Wildlife Federation. As a result, 65 percent of the plants used in those areas were natives; this included a large wildflower meadow and native crab apple orchard planted for wildlife. Private lots were certified as backyard wildlife habitats under the National Wildlife Federation's Certified Wildlife Habitat program. This certification program requires food, cover, and water for birds, butterflies, and other animals. To help insure that the builders who constructed homes on the development's lots kept biodiversity conservation in mind, the developers created site development guidelines. All builders had to submit a thousand-dollar construction deposit, and before construction could begin, they had to submit plans to an architecture review committee for approval. Also according to the guidelines, native plants were required; a twenty-to-fifty-foot natural vegetation buffer in the backyard had to be conserved; beyond fifteen feet from the foundations of homes, no trees could be removed that measured eight inches in diameter at breast height, without written approval from the architecture review committee; any protected tree that died within two years had to be replaced; natural drainage had to be respected and retained; and pervious pavement was strongly recommended. In addition, the guidelines provided a list of native plants and information about the wildlife habitat certification program.

Postconstruction: Signs discussing native landscaping in the neighborhood and plant identification plaques were installed in the common areas to raise awareness about natives. The CC&R addressed the intent of creating a wildlife-friendly community. In particular, the document has regulations regarding the conservation of natural areas and wildlife habitat: (1) it stipulates that natural drainage patterns must not affect wildlife habitats, (2) it references the site development guidelines and native plants list, (3) it requires that HOA dues help maintain the natural areas, signage, and native vegetation, and (4) it stipulates that pets must be on-leash when outside of homeowner lots. Real estate agents communicated to potential homebuyers the wildlife-friendly goal of the development, helped builders obtain wildlife habitat certification, and, once a home was sold, gave homeowners information about the certification, and educational materials about landscaping for wildlife. The postconstruction steps were important, as they helped to form a neighborhood norm concerning biodiversity conservation and the acceptance of native landscaping. As a testament to this, one homeowner, a year after she moved in, improved upon her landscaping and used a variety of native plants. She stated, "I love how the homes are tucked within the trees, and I thoroughly enjoy the natural areas that provide opportunities to walk and observe nature."

This particular development project happened because both the developer and the town staff had a vision of building a conservation subdivision. Because both parties had a similar vision, the exchanges among all parties facilitated the implementation of conservation-oriented design and management practices. As with

(Continued on page 172)

all subdivision projects, the Woodlands subdivision was a negotiation between town staff and the developer. These negotiations went well, but without informed town staff and a willing developer, the intent of a policy could be abused. Even when an open space policy is required by town ordinance, a developer may fight to divide a property's open space into small, isolated slivers, so that it is not contiguous; or a developer may leave very little native vegetation on the open space. Isolated patches have little value as wildlife habitat. And if significant trees and natural areas are conserved (at least on paper), heavy machinery and improper construction practices can heavily affect these areas, compromising their biological integrity.

Even with the enabling conditions at the town level and an engaged developer, the process at The Woodlands was not without challenges. For example, the developer proposed to construct swales, instead of curbs, pipes, and gutters, to convey stormwater. However, curb-and-gutter regulations were on the books at the time. According to the developer, the use of swales was initially somewhat difficult to get approved by the town. Planners associated with the project became advocates for this creative solution. As a result, a variance for the swales was passed, and subsequently a new LID ordinance was created. The project piloted the use of LID practices for future subdivisions. In addition, the goal of using native plants for landscaping was difficult because of a lack of native plant nurseries in the area. Despite this, the town planning firm and the developer located sources for native plants. Barriers will always be encountered when novel ideas are explored, but a supportive planning staff and a diligent developer will solve most problems. Although not all the design and management practices suggested in this book were used in this development, the project was unique for the area, and it is being held up as a model for future development. Such projects raise the bar and ultimately pave the way for even more creative solutions in the future.

NOTES

CHAPTER I. WHY BUILD BIODIVERSE COMMUNITIES?

1. United Nations Information Service. "UN Report Says World Urban Population of 3 Billion Today Expected to Reach 5 Billion by 2030." 2004, www.unis.unvienna .org/unis/pressrels/2004/pop899.html. The figures come from the United Nations Population Division.

2. Wackernagel, M., and R. William. 1996. *Our Ecological Footprint: Reducing Human Impact on the Earth.* Gabriola Island, BC: New Society Press.

3. Reid, S.K., and L.R. Oki. 2008. "Field trials identify more native plants suited to urban landscaping." *California Agriculture* 62(3): 97–104.

4. U.S. Environmental Protection Agency. 2009. "Storm water phase II final rule: Construction site runoff control minimum control measure." Rep. No. EPA 833/ F-00/008, Office of Water, Washington, DC.

5. Huang, Y.J., H. Akbari, H. Taha, and A.H. Rosenfeld. 1987. "The potential of vegetation in reducing summer cooling loads in residential buildings." *Journal of Climate and Applied Meteorology* 26(9): 1103–1116.

6. United Nations Information Service, "UN Report Says World Urban Population."

7. McKinney, M.L. 2002. "Urbanization, biodiversity, and conservation." *Bioscience* 52: 883–890.

8. Kellert, S.R. 1996. *The Value of Life: Biological Diversity and Human Society.* Washington, DC: Island Press.

9. Miller, J.R. 2005. "Biodiversity conservation and the extinction of experience." *Trends in Ecology and Evolution* 20(8): 430–434.

10. Kahn, P.H., Jr., and B. Friedman. 1995. "Environmental views and values of children in an inner-city black community." *Child Development* 66:1403–1417.

11. Williams, K.J.H., and J. Cary. 2002. "Landscape preferences, ecological quality, and biodiversity protection." *Environment and Behavior* 34:257–274.

12. Dale, V.H., F. Akhtar, M. Aldridge, L. Baskaran, M. Berry, M. Browne, M. Chang, M., R. Efroymson, C. Garten, E. Lingerfelt, and C. Stewart. 2008. "Modeling the effects of land use on the quality of water, air, noise, and habitat for a five-county region in Georgia." *Ecology and Society* 13(1): article no. 10.

13. Bell, C.E., J.M. DiTomaso, and C.A. Wilen. 2007. *Invasive plants: Integrated pest management around the home and landscape.* Pest Notes series. Davis: UC Statewide IPM Program, University of California, Davis. Available at www.ipm.ucdavis.edu/PMG/PESTNOTES/pn74139.html.

14. Lin, Y.J., Z.L. He, Y.G. Yang, P.J. Stoffella, E.J. Phlips, and C.A. Powell. 2008. "Nitrogen versus phosphorus limitation of phytoplankton growth in Ten Mile Creek, Florida, USA." *Hydrobiologia* 605:247–258.

15. Gannon, D.P., E.J.B. McCabe, S.A. Camilleri, J.G. Gannon, M.K. Brueggen, A.A. Barleycorn, V.I. Palubok, G.J. Kirkpatrick, and R.S. Wells. 2009. "Effects of *Karenia brevis* harmful algal blooms on nearshore fish communities in southwest Florida." *Marine Ecology, Progress Series,* 378:171–186.

16. Diaz, R.J., and R. Rosenberg. 2008. "Spreading dead zones and consequences for marine ecosystems." *Science* 321(5891): 926–929.

17. Sutton, D.L., T.K. Van, and K.M. Portier. 1992. "Growth of dioecious and monoecious hydrilla from single tubers." *Journal of Aquatic Plant Management* 30:15–20.

18. Adapted from Knowles, H., and M.E. Hostetler. 2005. *Preserving Wildlife Habitat in Residential Developments.* Gainesville: Program for Resource Efficient Communities, University of Florida.

19. Millennium Ecosystem Assessment. 2005. *Ecosystems and Human Well-Being: Synthesis.* Millennium Ecosystem Assessment Series. New York: Island Press.

20. Costanza, R., R. d'Arge, R.. de Groot, S. Farber, M. Grasso, B. Hannon, K. Limburg, S. Naeem, R.V. O'Neill, J. Paruelo, R.G. Raskin, P. Sutton, and M. van den Belt. 1997. "The value of the world's ecosystem services and natural capital." *Nature* 387:253–260.

21. Millennium Ecosystem Assessment, *Ecosystems and Human Well-Being.*

22. Buchmann, S.L., and G.P. Nabhan. 1996. *The Forgotten Pollinators.* Washington, DC: Island Press.

23. Sanford, M. 2003. *Pollination of Citrus by Honey Bees.* EDIS document RFAA092. Gainesville: Entomology and Nematology Department, Florida Cooperative Extension Service, Institute of Food and Agricultural Sciences, University of Florida. Available at http://edis.ifas.ufl.edu/AA092.

Sanford, M. 2003. *Protecting honey bees from pesticides.* EDIS circ. 534. Gainesville: Entomology and Nematology Department, Florida Cooperative Extension Service, Institute of Food and Agricultural Sciences, University of Florida. Available at http://edis.ifas.ufl.edu/document_aa145.

24. Buchmann and Nabhan, *The Forgotten Pollinators.*

25. Vaughan, M., and S.H. Black. 2006. "Agroforestry: Sustaining native bee habitat for crop pollination." *Agroforestry Notes* 32:1–4.

26. National Oceanic and Atmospheric Administration. 2002. *Historical Expenditures for Beach Nourishment Projects: Geographical Distribution of Projects and Sources of Funding,* www.csc.noaa.gov/beachnourishment/html/human/socio/geodist.htm.

27. Ludwig, D., D.D. Jones, and C.S. Holling. 1978. "Qualitative analysis of insect outbreak systems: The spruce budworm and forest." *Journal of Animal Ecology* 47:315–332.

28. Reich, P.B., J. Knops, D. Tilman, J. Craine, D. Ellsworth, M. Tjoelker, T. Lee, D. Wedin, S. Naeem, D. Bahauddin, G. Hendrey, S. Jose, K. Wrage, J. Goth, and W. Bengston. 2001. "Plant diversity enhances ecosystem responses to elevated CO_2 and nitrogen deposition." *Nature* 410(6830): 809–812.

29. Bixler, R.D., M.F. Floyd, and W.E. Hammitt. 2002. "Environmental socialization: Quantitative tests of the childhood play hypothesis." *Environment and Behavior* 34(6): 795–818.

30. Matsuoka, R.H., and R. Kaplan. 2008. "People needs in the urban landscape: Analysis of landscape and urban planning contributions." *Landscape and Urban Planning* 84(1): 7–19.

31. Kellert, S.R. 2005. *Building for Life: Designing and Understanding the Human-Nature Connection.* Washington, DC: Island Press.

32. Wilson, E.O., and S.R. Kellert. 1995. *The Biophilia Hypothesis.* Washington, DC: Island Press.

33. Ulrich, R.S., R.F. Simons, B.D. Losito, E. Fiorito, M.A. Miles, and M. Zelson. 1991. "Stress recovery during exposure to natural and urban environments." *Journal of Environmental Psychology* 11(3): 201–230.

34. Wells, N.M., and G.W. Evans. 2003. "Nearby nature: A buffer of life stress among rural children." *Environment and Behavior* 35:311–330.

35. Kaplan, R., and S. Kaplan. 1989. *The Experience of Nature: A Psychological Perspective.* New York: Cambridge University Press.

36. Moore, E.O. 1981. "A prison environment's effect on health care service demands." *Journal of Environmental Systems* 11:17–34.

37. Ulrich, R.S. 1984. "View through a window may influence recovery from surgery." *Science* 224:420–421.

38. Leyden, K. 2003. "Social capital and the built environment: The importance of walkable neighborhoods." *American Journal of Public Health* 93(9): 1546–1551.

39. Stedman, R.C. 2003. "Is it really just a social construction? The contribution of the physical environment to sense of place." *Society and Natural Resources* 16:671–685.

40. Benfield, K.F., M.D. Raimi, and D.D. Chen. 1999. *Once There Were Greenfields: How Urban Sprawl Is Undermining America's Environment, Economy, and Social Fabric.* New York: Natural Resource Defense Council.

41. Brown, B.B., J.R. Burton, and A.L. Sweaney. 1998. "Neighbors, households and front porches: New Urbanist community tool or mere nostalgia?" *Environment and Behavior* 30:579–601.

42. Matsuoka and Kaplan, *Landscape and Urban Planning.*

43. U.S. Fish and Wildlife Service. 2007. *2006 National Survey of Fishing, Hunting and Wildlife-Associated Recreation,* www.fws.gov.

44. Ibid.

45. Bowman, T., J. Thompson, and J. Colletti. 2009. "Valuation of open space and conservation features in residential subdivisions." *Journal of Environmental Management* 90(1): 321–330.

46. Noiseux, K., and M.E. Hostetler. 2010. "Eco-opportunity knocks: Do home-buyers want green features in communities?" *Environment and Behavior* 42(5): 551–580.

47. Mohamed, R. 2006. "The economics of conservation subdivisions: Price premiums, improvement costs, and absorption." *Urban Affairs Review* 41(3): 376–399.

48. Romero, M., and M.E. Hostetler. 2006. *Policies That Address Sustainable Building Practices.* EDIS circ. 1518. Gainesville: Wildlife Ecology and Conservation Department, Florida Cooperative Extension Service, Institute of Food and Agricultural Sciences, University of Florida. Available at http://edis.ifas.ufl.edu/UW252.

49. Di Giulio, M., R. Holdereggera, and S. Tobias. 2009. "Effects of habitat and landscape fragmentation on humans and biodiversity in densely populated landscapes." *Journal of Environmental Management* 90(10): 2959–2968.

50. Arendt, R.G. 1996. *Conservation Design for Subdivisions: A Practical Guide to Creating Open Space Networks.* Washington, DC: Island Press.

Odell, E.A., D.M. Theobald, and R.L. Knight. 2003. "A songbird's case for clustered housing developments." *Journal of American Planning Association* 69:1–15.

51. Theobald, D.M., J.R. Miller, and N.T. Hobbs. 1997. "Estimating the cumulative effects of development on wildlife habitat." *Landscape and Urban Planning* 39:25–36.

Till, K.E. 2001. "New Urbanism and nature: Green marketing and the neo-traditional community." *Urban Geography* 22:220–248.

52. Congress for the New Urbanism. 2007. *Charter of the New Urbanism.* Available at www.cnu.org/charter.

53. Hansen, A.J., R.L. Knight, J. Marzluff, S. Powell, K. Brown, P. Hernandez, and K. Jones. 2005. "Effects of exurban development on biodiversity: Patterns, mechanisms, research needs." *Ecological Application* 15:1893–1905.

Hostetler, M.E., S. Duncan, and J. Paul. 2005. "The effects of an apartment complex on migrating and wintering birds." *Southeastern Naturalist* 4: 421–434.

Lenth, B.A., R.L. Knight, and W.C. Gilgert. 2006. "Conservation value of clustered housing developments." *Conservation Biology* 20:1445–1456.

CHAPTER 2. URBAN DECISION MAKERS

1. Miller, J.R., M. Groom, G.R. Hess, T. Steelman, D.L. Stokes, J. Thompson, T. Bowman, L. Fricke, B. King, and R. Marquardt. 2009. "Biodiversity conservation in local planning." *Conservation Biology* 23(1): 53–63.

2. Honachefsky, W. 1999. *Ecologically Based Municipal Land Use Planning.* Boca Raton, FL: CRC Press.

3. Hometown Democracy Amendment, www.floridahometowndemocracy.com/, accessed 2009.

4. Youngentob, K., and M.E. Hostetler. 2005. "Is a new urban development model building greener communities?" *Environment and Behavior* 37:731–759.

5. Cialdini, Robert B. 1996. "Activating and aligning two kinds of norms in persuasive communications." *Journal of Interpretation Research* 1(1): 3–10 (Winter).

6. Leung, C., and J. Rice. 2002. "Comparison of Chinese-Australian and Anglo-Australian environmental attitudes and behaviors." *Social Behavior and Personality* 30(3): 251–262.

7. Hungerford, H.R. 1996. "The development of responsible environmental citizenship: A critical challenge." *Journal of Interpretation Research* 1(1): 25–37 (Winter).

8. Brown, B.B., J.R. Burton, and A.L. Sweaney. 1998. "Neighbors, households, and front porches: New Urbanist community toll or mere nostalgia?" *Environment and Behavior* 30:579–601.

9. Mesch, G.S., and O. Manor. 1998. "Social ties, environmental perception, and local attachment." *Environment and Behavior* 30(4): 504–520 (July).

PART 2. THE DEVIL IS IN THE DETAILS

1. Chen, D. 2000. "The science of smart growth." *Scientific American* 283:84–91.

2. Srinivasan, S., L.R. O'Fallon, and A. Dearry. 2003. "Creating healthy communities, healthy homes, healthy people: Initiating a research agenda on the built environment and public health." *American Journal of Public Health* 93(9): 1446–1450.

3. Hostetler, M.E. 2010. "Beyond design: The importance of construction and post-construction phases in green developments." *Sustainability* 2:1128–1137.

4. Hough, M. 1994. "Design with city nature: An overview of some issues." In *The Ecological City: Preserving and Restoring Urban Biodiversity*, edited by R.H. Platt, R.A. Rowntree, and P.C. Muick, pp. 40–48. Amherst: University of Massachusetts Press.

CHAPTER 3. TREE PROTECTION AND NATURAL AREA PRESERVATION STRATEGIES

1. American Forests. "Why It Matters." N.d., www.americanforests.org/why-it-matters, accessed 2011.

2. Ibid.

3. American LIVES. 1999. *1999 Community Preferences: What the Buyers Really Want in Design, Features and Amenities*, www.americanlives.com/.

4. Adams, C.E., K.J. Lindsey, and S.J. Ash. 2006. *Urban Wildlife Management*. Boca Raton, FL: CRC Press.

5. Ibid.

6. Miller, S.G., R.L. Knight, and C.K. Miller. 1998. "Influence of recreational trails on breeding bird communities." *Ecological Applications* 8(1): 162–169.

7. This section adapted from Knowles, H., and M.E. Hostetler. 2005. *Preserving Wildlife Habitat in Residential Developments*. Gainesville: Program for Resource Efficient Communities, University of Florida.

8. Yahner, R.H. 1988. "Changes in wildlife communities near edges." *Conservation Biology* 2:333–339.

9. Brand, L.A., and T.L. George. 2001. "Response of passerine birds to forest edge in coast redwood forest fragments." *The Auk* 118(3): 678–686.

10. Ibid.

11. Thompson, J.W., and K. Sorvig. 2008. *Sustainable Landscape Construction: A Guide to Green Building Outdoors.* 2nd ed. Washington, DC: Island Press.

12. Dube, R.L., and F.C. Campbell. 1999. *Natural Stonescapes: The Art and Craft of Stone Placement.* Pownal, VT: Storey Communications/Garden Way.

13. Adapted from Ruppert, K.C., C. White, P. Dessaint, E. Gilman, and E. Foreste. 2005. *Trees and Construction: Keeping Trees Alive in the Urban Forest.* Program for Resource Efficient Communities. University of Florida, Gainesville, FL.

14. Soehne, W. 1958. "Fundamentals of pressure distribution and soil compaction under tractor tires." *Agricultural Engineering* 39:276–281.

15. Schultz, R.C., J.P. Colletti, T.M. Isenhart, W.W. Simpkins, C.W. Mize, and M.L. Thompson. 1995. "Design and placement of a multi-species riparian buffer strip system." *Agroforestry Systems* 29(3): 201–226.

16. Desbonnet, A., P. Pogue, V. Lee, and N. Wolff. 1994. *Vegetated Buffers in the Coastal Zone—a Summary Review and Bibliography.* Coastal Resources Center Technical Report No. 2064. Narragansett, RI: University of Rhode Island Graduate School of Oceanography.

17. Chagrin River Watershed Partners. 2006. *Riparian Setbacks Technical Information for Decision Makers.* Available at www.crwp.org/pdf_files/riparian_setback_paper_jan_2006.pdf.

18. Conover, M.R. 2002. *Resolving Human-Wildlife Conflicts: The Science of Wildlife Damage Management.* New York: Lewis Publishers.

19. O'Donnell, M.A., and J.A. DeNicola. 2006. "Den site selection of lactating female raccoons following removal and exclusion from suburban residences." *Wildlife Society Bulletin* 34:366–370.

20. Beckman, J.P., and J. Berger. 2003. "Rapid ecological and behavioural changes in carnivores: The response of black bears (*Ursus americanus*) to altered food." *Journal of Zoology London* 26:207–212.

21. Smith, A.E., S.R. Craven, and P.D. Curtis. 1999. *Managing Canada Geese in Urban Environments.* Ithaca, NY: Jack Berryman Institute Publication 16 and Cornell University Cooperative Extension.

22. Smith, L.A., and P.I. Chow-Fraser. 2010. "Impacts of adjacent land use and isolation on marsh bird communities." *Environmental Management* 45(5): 1040–1051.

23. Hostetler, M.E., P. Jones, M. Dukes, H. Knowles, G. Acomb, and M. Clark. 2008. "With one stroke of the pen: How can extension professionals involve developers and policymakers in creating sustainable communities?" *Journal of Extension* 46(1). Available at www.joe.org.

24. Van der Leeden, F., F.L. Troise, and D.K. Todd. 1990. *The Water Encyclopedia.* 2nd ed. Chelsea, MI: Lewis Publishers.

25. McElfish, J.M., Jr. 2004. *Nature-Friendly Ordinances*. Washington, DC: Environmental Law Institute.

26. Land Use Code, Bellevue, Washington, 20.30D.160: Planned Unit Development Plan: Conservation Feature and Recreation Space Requirement.

27. Municipal Code Park City, Utah, Chapter 2.21: "Sensitive Land Overlay Zone (SLO) Regulations."

CHAPTER 4. IMPROVING COMMUNITY ENGAGEMENT AND UNDERSTANDING

1. Youngentob, K., and M.E. Hostetler. 2005. "Is a new urban development model building greener communities?" *Environment and Behavior* 37:731–759.

2. Hostetler, M.E., and K. Noiseux. 2010. "Are green residential developments attracting environmentally savvy homeowners?" *Landscape and Urban Planning* 94:234–243.

3. Lenth, B.A., R.L. Knight, and W.C. Gilgert. 2006. "Conservation value of clustered housing developments." *Conservation Biology* 20:1445–1456.

4. Austin, M.E. 2004. "Resident perspectives of the open space conservation subdivision in Hamburg Township, Michigan." *Landscape and Urban Planning* 69:245–253.

5. Cialdini, R.B. 1996. "Activating and aligning two kinds of norms in persuasive communications." *Journal of Interpretation Research* 1(1): 3–10.

6. McKenzie-Mohr, D., and W. Smith. 1999. *Fostering Sustainable Behavior*. Gabriola Island, Canada: New Society.

7. Peine, J.D. 2001. "Nuisance bears in communities: Strategies to reduce conflict." *Human Dimensions of Wildlife* 6(3): 223–237.

8. Smith, A.E., S.R. Craven, and P.D. Curtis. 1999. *Managing Canada Geese in Urban Environments*. Ithaca, NY: Jack Berryman Institute Publication 16 and Cornell University Cooperative Extension.

9. Noiseux, K., and M. E. Hostetler. 2010. "Eco-opportunity knocks: Do homebuyers want green features in communities?" *Environment and Behavior* 42(5): 551–580.

10. Hostetler, M.E., E. Swiman, A. Prizzia, and K. Noiseux. 2008. "Reaching residents of green communities: Evaluation of a unique environmental education program." *Applied Environmental Education and Communication* 7:114–124.

11. Ibid.

12. McKenzie-Mohr and Smith. *Fostering Sustainable Behavior*.

CHAPTER 5. LANDSCAPING AND INDIVIDUAL LOTS

1. Adapted from M. E. Hostetler. 1997. *That Gunk on Your Car: A Unique Guide to Insects of North America*. Berkeley, CA: Ten Speed Press.

2. Lewis, C.A. 1996. *Green Nature/Human Nature: The Meaning of Plants in Our Lives*. Champaign, IL: University of Illinois Press.

3. Jenkins, V.S. 1994. *The Lawn: A History of an American Obsession*. Washington, DC: Smithsonian Books.

4. Ibid.

5. Ibid.

6. American Association for the Advancement of Science. 2006. *AAAS Board Statement on Climate Change.* www.aaas.org/news/press_room/climate_change/.

7. Ibid.

8. Townsend-Small, A., and C.I. Czimczik. 2010. "Carbon sequestration and greenhouse gas emissions in urban turf." *Geophysical Research Letters* 37: L02707.

9. Hostetler, M.E., and F. Escobedo. 2010. *What Types of Urban Greenspace Are Better for Carbon Dioxide Sequestration?* EDIS document WEC279. Gainesville: Wildlife Ecology and Conservation Department, Florida Cooperative Extension Service, Institute of Food and Agricultural Sciences, University of Florida. Available at http://edis.ifas.ufl.edu/uw324.

10. MacGregor-Fors, I. 2008. "Relation between habitat attributes and bird richness in a western Mexico suburb." *Landscape and Urban Planning* 84(1): 92–98.

11. Collinge, S.K., K.L. Prudic, and J.C. Oliver. 2003. "Effects of local habitat characteristics and landscape context on grassland butterfly diversity." *Conservation Biology* 17(1): 178–187.

12. McIntyre, N., and M.E. Hostetler. 2001. "Effects of urban land use on pollinator (Hymenoptera: Apodidea) communities in a desert metropolis." *Journal of Applied and Theoretical Biology* 2:209–218.

13. Mazzotti, F.J., W. Ostrenko, and A.T. Smith. 1981. "Effects of the exotic plants *Melaleuca quinquenervia* and *Casuarina equisetifolia* on small mammal populations in the eastern Florida Everglades." *Florida Scientist* 44(2): 65–71.

14. Invasive Species Specialist Group. "*Neyraudia reynaudiana* (Grass)." N.d. *Global Invasive Species Database,* www.issg.org, accessed 2009.

15. Ingold, D.J. 1994. "Influence of nest-site competition between European starlings and woodpeckers." *Wilson Bulletin* 106:227–241.

16. Wyatt, J.L., and E.A. Forys. 2004. "Conservation implications of predation by Cuban Treefrogs (*Osteopilus septentrionalis*) on native hylids in Florida." *Southeastern Naturalist* 3(4): 695–700.

17. American Bird Conservancy. N.d. "Domestic Cat Predation on Birds and Other Wildlife," www.abcbirds.org, accessed 2009.

18. Michael, C., S. Thomasa, S., Bradleya, and H. McCutcheon. 2007. "Reducing the rate of predation on wildlife by pet cats: The efficacy and practicability of collar-mounted pounce protectors." *Biological Conservation* 137(3): 341–48.

19. Blewett, C.M, and J.M. Marzluff. 2005. "Effects of urban sprawl on snags and the abundance and productivity of cavity-nesting birds." *Condor* 107(3): 678–693.

20. Mills, G.S., J.B.J. Dunning, and J.M. Bates. 1989. "Effects of urbanization on breeding bird community structure in southwestern desert habitats." *The Condor* 91:416–428.

21. Hostetler, M.E., and C.S. Holling. 2000. "Detecting the scales at which birds respond to landscape structure in urban landscapes." *Urban Ecosystems* 4:25–54.

22. Chiras, D., and D. Wann. 2003. *Superbia!: 31 Ways to Create Sustainable Neighborhoods.* Gabriola Island, Canada: New Society Publishers.

23. Scalise, K. 1998. "Californians pay huge bill to keep their yards, landscaping beautiful, according to UC Berkeley report." University of California, Berkeley. Available at http://berkeley.edu/news/media/releases/98legacy/11–23–1998a.html.

24. Adapted from University of Florida/IFAS Extension. 2009. *The Florida Yards and Neighborhoods Handbook*. Available at Florida-Friendly Landscaping, fyn.ifas.ufl.edu/.

CHAPTER 6. TRAILS, SIDEWALKS, AND COMMON AREAS

1. Youngentob, K., and M.E. Hostetler. 2005. "Is a new urban development model building greener communities?" *Environment and Behavior* 37:731–759.

Lund, H. 2002. "Pedestrian environments and sense of community." *Journal of Planning Education and Research* 21(3): 301–312.

2. Hostetler, M.E., E. Swiman, A. Prizzia, and K. Noiseux. 2008. "Reaching residents of green communities: Evaluation of a unique environmental education program." *Applied Environmental Education and Communication* 7:114–124.

3. Frank, L.D., B.E. Saelens, K.E. Powell, and J.E. Chapman. 2007. "Stepping towards causation: Do built environments or neighborhood and travel preferences explain physical activity, driving, and obesity?" *Social Science and Medicine* 65(9): 1898–1914.

4. National Park Service. 1995. *Economic Impacts of Protecting Rivers, Trails, and Green Corridors*. 4th ed. Available at www.nps.gov/pwro/rtca/econ_index.htm.

5. Krasny, M., and R. Doyle. 2002. "Participatory approaches to program development and engaging youth in research: The case of an inter-generational urban community gardening program." *Journal of Extension* 40(5), www.joe.org/joe/2002october/a3.php.

6. Romero, M., and M.E. Hostetler. 2006. *Policies That Address Sustainable Building Practices*. EDIS circ. 1518. Gainesville: University of Florida. Available at http://edis.ifas.ufl.edu/UW252.

CHAPTER 7. IRRIGATION AND STORMWATER TREATMENT

1. Haley, M.B., M.D. Dukes, and G. L. Miller. 2007. "Residential irrigation water use in Central Florida." *Journal of Irrigation and Drainage Engineering* 133(5): 427–434.

2. N. Crabbe. 2007. "Health risk from springs' pollution not fully known." *Gainesville Sun*, May 13, www.gainesville.com/article/20070513/LOCAL/705130312.

R. Littlepage. 2005. "Toxic algae bloom on river calls for serious action." *Florida-Times Union*, August 25, www.jacksonville.com/tu-online/stories/082505/opl_19586308.shtml.

3. Pearce, F. 2006. *When the Rivers Run Dry: Water: The Defining Crisis of the Twenty-first Century*. Boston, MA: Beacon Press.

4. "New water rules impacting development take effect." 2007. *South Florida Business Journal*, April 3, http://southflorida.bizjournals.com/southflorida/stories/2007/04/02/daily14.html.

5. The Florida Council of 100. 2003. *Improving Florida's Water Supply Management Structure*. Tampa: The Florida Council of 100. Available at www.fc100.org/documents/waterreportfinal.pdf.

6. Youngentob, K., and M.E. Hostetler. 2005. "Is a new urban development model building greener communities?" *Environment and Behavior* 37:731–759.

7. Dr. Mark Clark, University of Florida. Personal communication, 2008.

8. Galli, J. 1992. *Preliminary Analysis of the Performance and Longevity of Urban BMPs Installed in Prince George's County, Maryland*. Largo, MD: Prince George's County, Maryland, Department of Natural Resources.

9. *Stormwater Management Fact Sheet: Porous Pavement*. N.d., www.stormwater center.net, accessed 2008.

10. McCready, M.S., M.D. Dukes, and G.L. Miller. 2009. "Water conservation potential of smart irrigation controllers on St. Augustine grass." *Agricultural Water Management* 96(11): 1623–1632.

11. Trenholm, L.E., J.B. Unruh, and J.L. Cisar. 2001. *Mowing Your Florida Lawn*. EDIS document ENH10. Gainesville: Environmental Horticulture Department, Florida Cooperative Extension Service, Institute of Food and Agricultural Sciences, University of Florida. Available at http://edis.ifas.ufl.edu/LH028.

12. EPA. 2007. *Reducing Stormwater Costs through Low Impact Development (LID) Strategies and Practices*. Washington, DC: Environmental Protection Agency. Available at www.epa.gov/nps/lid.

13. Haman, D.Z., and F.T. Izuno. 2003. *Principles of Micro Irrigation*. EDIS document AE70. Gainesville: Agricultural and Biological Engineering Department, Florida Cooperative Extension Service, Institute of Food and Agricultural Sciences, University of Florida. Available at http://edis.ifas.ufl.edu/WI007.

14. Gregory, J.H., M.D. Dukes, P.H. Jones, and G.L. Miller. 2006. "Effect of urban soil compaction on infiltration rate." *Journal of Soil and Water Conservation* 61(3): 117–124.

15. Rouse, R.E., Miavitz, E.M., and F.M. Roka. 2010. *Guide to Using Rhizomal Perennial Peanut in the Urban Landscape*. EDIS document HS960. Gainesville: Horticultural Sciences Department, Florida Cooperative Extension Service, Institute of Food and Agricultural Sciences, University of Florida. Available at http://edis.ifas.ufl.edu/EP135.

CHAPTER 8. WILDLIFE-FRIENDLY TRANSPORTATION SYSTEMS

1. The guidelines are taken in part from Burden, D., M. Wallwork, K. Sides, R. Trias, R., and H.B. Rue. 1999. *Street Design Guidelines for Healthy Neighborhoods*. Sacramento, CA: Center for Livable Communities.

2. Rich, C., and T. Longcore, eds. 2005. *Ecological Consequences of Artificial Night Lighting*. Washington, DC: Island Press.

3. William Ruediger. 2001. "High, wide, and handsome: Designing more effective wildlife and fish crossings for roads and highways," in *Proceedings of the 2001*

International Conference on Ecology and Transportation, ed. C.L. Irwin, P. Garrett, and K.P. McDermott. Raleigh, NC: Center for Transportation and the Environment, North Carolina State University, see http://repositories.cdlib.org/jmie/roadeco/ Reudiger2001a/.

1000 Friends of Florida. 2008. "Planning for Transportation Facilities and Wild-life." In *Wildlife: Wildlife Habitat Planning Strategies, Design Features and Best Management Practices for Florida Communities and Landowners,* http://floridahabitat.org/ wildlife-manual/transportation.

CHAPTER 10. CERTIFYING GREEN COMMUNITIES

1. Schendler, A., and R. Udall. 2005. *LEED Is Broken . . . Let's Fix It.* N.d. Alpen Snowmass. Available at www.aspensnowmass.com/environment/images/LEEDis Broken.pdf.

2. Ibid.

3. Ibid.

INDEX

agricultural land: cattle grazing, 85; as conservation easements, 57–59; focusing development on, 43–44

agriculture: impact of global climate change on, 94; pollinator population decline, 11; water polluted by, 116

air pollution: traffic and, 139; trees to reduce, 37–38. *See also* global climate change

algal blooms, water pollution and, 7, 40–41

alligators, conflicts with humans, 65, 149

American Bird Conservancy, Cats Indoors Campaign, 98

American Community Garden Association, 113

aquatic animals: killed by water pollution, 7; limiting construction during activity times, 66; wildlife corridors for, 144

arborists, to protect conserved trees, 62–63, 75

ardesia, coral, 97

Arizona: desert landscaping policies, 40, 147–48; water diversion projects, 117

asphalt. *See* impervious surfaces

Audubon International, green community certification, 158

Australia, Aurora community, 60–61

Australian pine, 97

barriers to green development, xiii–xiv; CC&Rs, 148–49;,economic, xiv; identifying, 87–89; social/cultural attitudes, 31, 90–91, 163–65, 167. *See also* funding

barriers to green development, political or governmental, xiv; identifying, 108–9, 114–15;

LID practices, 130; strategies for combating, 168, 170, 172; wildlife-friendly transportation systems, 145

bats, conflicts with humans, 64

bears, conflicts with humans, 38, 64, 82, 149

bees: native, 96; as pollinators, 11, 12–13

beetle, big sand tiger, 88

bicycles, as alternative transportation, 138–39, 145. *See also* paths, trails, and walkways

BioBlitz, Connecticut, 88–89

biocapacity, defined, 5–6

biodiversity: components of, 3–4; defined, 3, 4; distinguished from species richness, 4; ecosystem diversity, 3; ecosystem services and, 10–13; genetic diversity, 4, 11, 12–13; of pollinators, 11; of restored vs. conserved patches, 54; species diversity, 3, 12–13. *See also* urban biodiversity

biodiversity conservation: benefits of, xii; in green communities, 17–18; land development regulations and, 22–23; natural resource consumption and, 6; policy maker roles, 21; resident roles, 28–29

biological controls, specified in CC&Rs, 150

bioretention, LID and, 119–20, 121

birds: artificial lighting and, 141–42; Audubon International certification, 158; community monitoring projects, 14–15, 85; conflicts with humans, 38, 64–65, 82; insect control by, 12, 100–101; killed by pets, 98, 100; limiting construction during times of significant activity, 66; native species replaced by exotics, 98;

TEXT
10.5/14 Jenson Pro

DISPLAY
Jenson Pro

COMPOSITOR
BookComp, Inc.

INDEXER
Ellen Sherron

PRINTER AND BINDER
IBT Global